Robert Burns, Poet
born 1759

cover illustrations
by
Margaret Irving Miller

The
Burns Supper
Companion

by Hugh Douglas

© Alloway Publishing, 1998

ISBN 0-907526-74-8

Reprinted, 2003

Printed in Scotland by
Walker & Connell Ltd., Hastings Square, Darvel, Ayrshire.

THE BURNS SUPPER COMPANION
CONTENTS

FOREWORD

'Scotland is tremendously earnest in all that relates to Burns: in earnest alike her gratitude and her penitence'.

Punch *comment following the great celebration of Robert Burns at Alloway in 1844.*

Let's admit it right from the start, we *are earnest* about Robert Burns. And we are *grateful* to him and *penitent* about our treatment of him during his lifetime. Since his death, however, his memory has fared considerably better.

The anniversary of his birth, 25 January, is Scotland's big night. And the world's too. That's Burns Night, the night on which we honour Robert Burns, a man whose poetry is enjoyed and relates to our lives today as closely as it did when he lived among us, sharing the joys, sorrows and hardships of common folk more than two centuries ago. To mark his birthday, on 25 January every year, dinners are held all round the world with haggis served as the centrepiece of the bill of fare, and toasts are drunk to his memory - the Immortal Memory. They call these gatherings Burns Suppers, or for sticklers of formality, Anniversary Dinners, but whatever name is used, the format is much the same everywhere. The chief ingredients of this uniquely Scottish event are haggis, plenty of Burns's poetry, maybe a dram or two, and good comradeship.

But every year many people find themselves attending a Burns Supper for the first time, and proposing the Immortal Memory, giving the toast to the lassies, addressing the haggis, or organising the entire evening, This book is a lifeline thrown to all who find themselves in that position, but it has also been written for the enjoyment of regular Burns Supper-goers to remind them of past enjoyments and savour the tradition that makes Burns Night such an important occasion on the Scottish calendar. Enjoy the book, but better still, find a Burns Supper to enjoy next 25 January and revel in the real thing.

To strangers, Burns Night holds many mysteries: it is a highly formalised, almost ritualistic celebration, which follows the same pattern in Melbourne, Minnesota, Moscow, aye or Alloway itself, the Ayrshire village where Burns was born. But within its basic formality it can incorporate infinite variety to make each Burns Night celebration a unique tribute to the genius of Scotland's favourite son. This formal pattern laid down by tradition can be daunting to the uninitiated, for to stray from the set rules or fail to add a proper Burns dimension to the evening brings down the wrath of many Burnsians.

As the world moves on, it becomes even more apparent that what Robert Burns has to say is as relevant today as ever. His words still ring true, so it is more than ever appropriate that we should pause for one evening in the year and remember this man who can still speak to all of us - kings or commoners - as few others can.

Many people have asked me to include more about the Poet in this new edition, so I have incorporated a broader picture of Burns's life and the tradition of the Burns Supper. I hope this will give pleasure as well as providing useful information to all who read it.

I am once again grateful to Allan Ramsay, Drew Stevenson and Donald MacDonald for assistance and advice. Jo Macsween of the Edinburgh haggis-making firm has given me a fine insight into this centrepiece of the evening, and I reproduce F. Marian McNeill's haggis recipe from her book *The Scots Kitchen* with permission of the publishers, Mercat Press. I am grateful to Clarissa Dickson Wright for permission to quote from her delightful book *The Haggis - A Little History*. All Burns quotations used are taken from the text of *The Complete Works of Robert Burns* edited by James Mackay published by Alloway Publishing. The Robert Burns World Federation (the Burns Federation), which does a splendid job fostering interest in Burns, has given me assistance on a number of points, and I thank John Inglis and Shirley Bell, its Chief Administrator. Sheena Andrew of the Carnegie Library, Ayr, has answered a number of queries, and staff of my local library and bookshop, Peterborough Central Library and Hammick's Bookshop, Peterborough, have both helped with information, My thanks to all of them.

I trust this book will unlock the door to the mysteries of Burns Night and be of help to those who are organising the evening's celebrations, proposing a toast, or merely attending as a guest. Above all, I hope it will tempt many to go back to reading the Poet's works, for enjoying Burns's poetry is what being a Burns enthusiast is all about.

HUGH DOUGLAS

Dedicated to
all the trusty souls
who will brave the 'Janwar win'
to honour our national bard
~ Robert Burns

HOW IT ALL BEGAN

Don't take my word for it; Robert Burns said it himself - haggis is an appropriate dish to serve to any hungry man, the stuff that made Ayrshire farmers the men they were in Burns's day. It gave them the strength to till and harvest the dour Ayrshire soil and persuade it to yield the food they needed to keep them and their families alive.

But mark the Rustic, haggis-fed,
    The trembling earth resounds his tread,
Clap in his walie* nieve a blade,   * large
    He'll mak it whissle;
An' legs, an' arms, an' heads will sned*,   * cut off
    Like taps o' thrissle*.   * thistle

Ye Pow'rs wha mak mankind your care,
    And dish them out their bill o' fare,
Auld Scotland wants nae skinking* ware,   * watery/thin
    That jaups in luggies*,   * milk pail
But, if ye wish her gratefu' pray'r,
    Gie her a Haggis!

It's only right then that a haggis should be the focal point of a dinner to celebrate Burns, a Scotsman above all our race and a poet above common poets. And of course it needs a dram to wash it down, and good company to complete the evening. A Burns Supper, held each year on 25 January, the anniversary of the Poet's birthday, should incorporate all these elements.

The Burns Supper tradition began purely by chance, After Robert Burns died on July 21, 1796, many people felt they couldn't sever the bond with this man whose poetry affected them so deeply, and one way of maintaining this link with his memory was to visit the cottage at Alloway in which he was born. The little house, built by Burns's father, had already been sold during the poet's lifetime to the Incorporation of Shoemakers of Ayr, who let it out to one of their members, and he turned it into an ale-house. Naturally, visitors were warmly welcomed at the cottage for their custom as well as their love of the Poet. On the anniversary of Burns's birthday in 1801, a number of non-commissioned officers and privates of the Argyll Militia, then stationed at Ayr, marched out to Alloway, where the regiment's band played 'a number of appropriate airs,' and no doubt sampled plenty of the innkeeper's ale. The only trouble was they were four days late - they made their pilgrimage on January 29, which everyone believed at that time to be the Poet's birth date, simply because James Currie, the first biographer, gave the 29th as the date of Burns's birth.

That same year the first recorded Burns Supper took place at Alloway, not on the date of his birth, but around the anniversary of his death in July. That summer a group of nine friends of Rab met at the cottage and sat down to 'a comfortable dinner of which sheep's head and haggis formed an interesting part.' The haggis was addressed just as is done at Suppers today, and when the meal was over, the Rev. Hamilton Paul made a speech praising the Poet, the first Immortal Memory. Every toast that day was drunk 'three times three times', that is to say nine times. One can only hope they didn't have as many toasts as are sometimes proposed at today's celebrations!

Among the nine present to drink the three times three toasts were Dr Partick Douglas of Garallan and two men who had helped to bring Burns to the notice of the world of Ayrshire and beyond, Provost John Ballantine of Ayr, and 'Orator' Bob Aiken, whom Burns called his 'first kind patron'.

Pace all those men who disapprove of women attending Burns Suppers (and they may be a dying breed, but there are still a few around), also present was Primrose Kennedy of Drumellan.

The Burns enthusiasts held their next dinner in January on the birth anniversary, or rather on the date on which they thought it fell, and for the next seven years they celebrated the Poet alternately in July and January. It was only in 1809 that it was decided to settle for a winter celebration.

And so the Burns Supper tradition was born.

All through the year pilgrims continued to visit the Alloway ale-house in ever increasing numbers, and were welcomed with enthusiasm for their bar custom rather that for their enthusiasm for Burns. When the poet John Keats visited Alloway in 1822, he was so angered that he described the landlord, 'Miller' Goudie, as 'a mahogany-faced old jackass who knew Burns; he drinks glasses five for the quarter, and twelve for the hour'. And Keats complained afterwards 'the dull dog made me write a dull sonnet.'

Greenock claims the honour of being the oldest Burns Club, with its origins dating back to July, 1801, the year the Argyll Fencibles marched out to the cottage with their band and Burns's friends met for the first time, They claim their first anniversary dinner was held on 29 January, 1802, but alas the club's first minute book, which would confirm this, has disappeared. Contesting Greenock's claim is Paisley Burns Club, whose pedigree goes back to 1805 with a minute book extant to prove it. Kilmarnock club followed only three years later in 1808, and from then on the Burns movement grew rapidly and the Burns Supper tradition became firmly established.

Throughout the nineteenth century Burns clubs proliferated until, in 1885, they were brought together into the Burns Federation. With headquarters in Kilmarnock, where the first edition of Burns' poems was printed and published, the Federation continues to work towards its original goal 'to strengthen and consolidate by universal affiliation the bond of fellowship existing amongst the members of Burns Clubs and kindred societies.' For details of the Robert Burns World Federation see Page 91.

THE MAN AND THE POET

1759 Robert Burns was born on . . . well let him tell you himself as he did with so many of the facts of his life . . .

> *Our monarch's hindmost year but ane[1]*
> *Was five-and-twenty days begun,*
> *'Twas then a blast o' Janwar Win'*
> *Blew hansel* in on Robin.*   * first gift

He was born in the cottage at Alloway, near Ayr, which has been preserved as a museum, looking very much as it was on 25 January, 1759, when Rab Burns first saw the light of day. He was the first child of William Burnes[2], who originally hailed from Kincardineshire in North East Scotland, and his wife, Agnes Broun, an Ayrshire lass. In the poem in which Robert told us of his birth he summed up his later life more succinctly than anyone has done since - He said he would grow into a roving lad with an eye for the girls, but we would be proud of him . . .

> *He'll hae misfortunes great and sma'*
> *But ay a heart aboon* them a';*   * above
> *He'll be a credit till us a',*
> *We'll a be proud o' Robin!*

When Robert's father took over the land at Alloway there was no house on it, so he had to build a shelter for himself and his wife with his own hands. When the cottage was ready he installed Agnes in it and began to cultivate the land as a market garden. Life was hard, and although the Burnes family were able to live every bit as well as other folk of their

---

[1] 1759, the last year of King George III's reign.
[2] Robert was the first to spell the name Burns without the 'e'.

kind, William sought more for his family. He joined with several neighbours to hire a tutor jointly to teach their children, and in 1765 took a lease on a larger farm.

1766 Burnes moved to the farm of Mount Oliphant a few miles inland, but soon ran into financial difficulties because he was unable to dispose of the lease of the Alloway cottage and the soil of Mount Oliphant proved poor and stony. Against all the odds William toiled on, and Robert and his brother, although still children, had to help on the farm. It was in the harvest field at Mount Oliphant that young Robert first fell in love - with a girl called Nell Kilpatrick - and Nell was the girl who first drove him to commit 'the sin of verse.'.

> *O once I lov'd a bonie lass,*
> *Ay, and I love her still!*
> *And whilst that virtue warms my breast,*
> *I'll love my handsome Nell.*

1775 During this summer Robert spent some weeks in school at Kirkoswald, near Maybole, but here another lassie drove study out of his mind. Peggy Thomson must have made a deep impression on the boy for he sent her a specially inscribed copy of his first book of poems . . .

> *Once fondly lov'd, and still remember'd dear,*
> *Sweet early object of my youthful vows.*

1777 William Burnes escaped from the bondage of Mount Pleasant at last to another farm, Lochlie, a couple of miles from Tarbolton, but this proved no more successful. The rent was high, and the land so boggy and wet that all the hard work of William Burnes, Robert and his second son, Gilbert, could make nothing of it. However, Lochlie brought one great advantage for Robert - it was near Tarbolton and it took him into contact with other young people. He joined the Tarbolton freemasons and found lads of his own age with whom he could argue, discuss the world around them and drink, There were lassies too, with whom he learnt to dance and flirt or even make love. He fell for Alison Begbie, but she jilted him, a painful experience for a lad accustomed to sweeping every girl he met off her feet.

1781 In this year Robert went to Irvine to learn the trade of flax-dressing, but that did not work out and he became ill and had to return home the following year.

1784 Following a distressing lawsuit over the tenancy of Lochlie William Burnes died, leaving Robert head of the family, a heavy burden for a young man just turned 25. But he faced up to it squarely and even after success as a poet took him away from the family, he continued to support them to the extent of depriving himself of an easy life. He and his brother Gilbert feared their father might lose everything if the Lochlie lawsuit went against him so they had taken a lease of another farm, Mossgiel, near Mauchline, just before their father died. By now Rab Burns had begun to catch the public's eye, first as the father of servant girl Lizzie Paton's illegitimate daughter, then as a rebel against narrowness and hypocrisy in the Church, and thirdly as a poet with a sharp pen to satirise faults within the Kirk and the failings of his fellow men, especially those who had treated his father and his family so harshly. Soon the kirk had more to complain about: another local girl Jean Armour became pregnant and Burns found himself so hotly pursued by the Mauchline minister, the Rev. William Auld, 'Daddy Auld' folk called him, and by Jean's father, that he thought seriously of emigrating to Jamaica to escape. Fortunately for us he changed his mind and remained in Scotland.

1786 This was a momentous year for the young rhymer of Mossgiel. In July John Wilson, a Kilmarnock printer, published a little book containing three dozen of Burns's poems. He printed 612 copies of *Poems Chiefly in the Scottish Dialect*, and within weeks the whole countryside was ablaze with talk about Robert Burns. The rich rushed to purchase it; so did servant men and girls who could ill afford the three shillings to buy a copy, and soon Burns's fame had spread to Edinburgh, but by then there was not a copy to be had.

1786 Autumn Burns went to Edinburgh to arrange for a second volume of his poems to be published, and spent a convivial winter in that dizzy - and so different - world. He met many of Scotland's richest and most influential men, and was accepted by a social club of lawyers, known as the Crochallan Fencibles, who drank at the Anchor Tavern. While in Edinburgh he was persuaded to sell the copyright of his book to an Edinburgh publisher, William Creech, for 100 guineas. Creech was a mean man who drove a hard bargain, and it took some considerable time for the poet to receive his money. By the following spring Robert had had enough of the narrow world of the capital and felt the need to escape.

1787 This was the year when Robert Burns saw Scotland. He made three tours of the country that year, one to the Borders and two to the Highlands. The Borders tour had a purpose - he wanted to look at a farm near Dumfries of which he had been offered a lease, but even after seeing it he could not make up his mind, so returned to Edinburgh disappointed. During the summer he travelled through the West Highlands and then the Highlands, travelling through Fife, Clackmannan, Stirlingshire and Perthshire to Inverness, as far north as Culloden. He enjoyed seeing his home country, but realised that decisions were going to have to be made - and not just about the farm.

1787-88 Robert visited Mauchline briefly and again met Jean Armour who had borne him twins during his absence, and who as a result of his return, was soon pregnant again. To his dying day, Burns had an eye for a girl, and too often these affairs ended in the same way. It was rumoured that 'Highland Mary' Campbell died bearing his child and the West Highland tour was made to visit her grave, but he himself said he made the journey to collect subscriptions for his book of poems. Meg Cameron and Jenny Clow in Edinburgh, and Anna Park in Dumfries all bore him children, but Agnes Maclehose, 'Clarinda', of his passionate affair in Edinburgh during the winter of 1787-88, kept him at arm's length, although she did inspire one of his loveliest songs:

> *Ae fond kiss, and then we sever!*
> *Ae farewell, and then forever!*
> *Deep in heart-wrung tears I'll pledge thee,*
> *Warring sighs and groans I'll wage thee.*

On his return to Mauchline in the spring of 1788 he and Jean were married, quietly and without anyone knowing. Nobody was ever sure when the marriage took place, but it was full of deep love as is shown so clearly by his poem, *O Were I on Parnassus Hill*, written only a few months later.

> *Then come, sweet Muse, inspire my lay!*
> *For a' the lee-lang* simmer's day*   *live-long
> *I couldna sing, I couldna say,*
> *How much, how dear I love thee.*
> *I see thee dancing o'er the green,*
> *Thy waist sae jimp*, thy limbs sae clean,*   *neat
> *Thy tempting lips, thy roguish een-*
> *By Heaven and Earth I love thee!*

In spite of all the problems life brought and all the other women in his life, Jean remained faithful to him to the end of his days and bore him nine children, the last born on the day of her husband's funeral. Jean was an inspiration, and we have to thank her for more than a dozen songs, of which the most moving is that timeless gem of a love song *Of a' the Airts:*

Of a' the airts the wind can blaw
I dearly like the west,
For there the bonie lassie lives,
The lassie I lo'e best.
There wild woods grow, and rivers row
And monie a hill between,
But day and night my fancy's flight
Is ever wi my Jean.

I see her in the dewy flowers-
I see her sweet and fair.
I hear her in the tunefu hirds-
I hear her charm the air.
There's not a bonie flower that springs
By fountain, shaw, or green,
There's not a bonie bird that sings,
But minds me o my Jean.

Soon after Jean became his wife, Robert decided to accept the lease of Ellisland, a farm beside the river Nith some six miles south of Dumfries. The land here was in poor heart and, as his father had found at Alloway, there was no farmhouse, so he had to set to and build a house for his new wife and family. Robert's luck in farming was very similar to that of his father, but his problems were compounded by the fact that he had been too generous to his family at Mossgiel, helping them to keep afloat, but at great sacrifice to himself. He hadn't enough capital to set himself up properly in Ellisland, so he had soon to take a job with the Excise Service to eke out the bare living the farm was yielding. Now he rode two hundred miles a week carrying out his Excise duties, yet still managed to tame the dour earth of Ellisland, but the strain told on his health and he was glad eventually to be able to rid himself of the farm and move into Dumfries.

1791 In Dumfries the family settled into a cramped flat on the second floor of a house in the Wee Vennel (now Bank Street) and Robert continued with his Excise work.

Always anxious to speak up for the poor and downtrodden, he thought highly of the French revolutionaries in the early days before the Revolution turned into a blood-bath. In a typical Burns gesture he bought four small guns from a captured ship and sent them off to France, but they were intercepted at Dover. When the Revolution became a brutal business and war broke out between France and Britain, however, his loyalty drove him to help to establish the Dumfries Volunteers, a local regiment raised to fend off the invasion that was then feared. He served with the Volunteers in addition to his hard Excise work, and the demands of it all took its toll on his health.

1793 This year he made another move, this time to a fine sandstone house in Mill Street (now called Burns Street) which is now a Burns Museum. From here he continued his Excise work, although these were difficult times because an Exciseman's earnings depended on imports, and imports dropped drastically during the war. As his income fell, Robert's financial problems increased, and he often became depressed and ill. As a result he quarrelled with some of his best friends and nearly fell foul of his Excise masters in Edinburgh.

1796 This year began badly: money was desperately tight by now, Jean was pregnant again, and a local tailor was dunning him for payment for his Volunteer uniform - it all preyed on Robert's mind, and he became ill once more. As a cure, his doctor sent him to Brow on the Solway Firth to bathe in the sea, but far from curing him, this hastened his death. He returned to Dumfries, to all his problems - and to certain death.

21st July, 1796 Robert Burns died, fearful for his family's future to the last.

25th July, 1796 They gave him a splendid funeral. Fellow Volunteers carried the coffin in procession to St Michael's Kirkyard, a military band played and soldiers fired a volley over the coffin as he was buried. And that same morning Jean gave birth to another son. She named him Maxwell after the doctor who had attended her husband during his last days and advised him to try the sea-bathing at Brow which hastened his death.

1796-1800 Robert Burns's fears for his family proved unfounded for friends began at once to raise a fund for Jean and the children, then another book of his poems was published, and from that moment the family never risked being in want. What is heartwarming is not just that people rallied to give a few shillings or pounds to his widow, but that his stature as a poet grew and has continued to do so ever since.

He had given the world a breathtaking variety of poems, from those brilliant, incisive satires against the hypocrisy he saw around him to that matchless, joyous epic *Tam O' Shanter*. He wrote poems sympathetic to nature all round him, yet summing up man's inhumanity to his fellow man and the consequent suffering. When he wrote of the mouse's suffering, he was writing of his own and every other man's anguish . . .

> *The best-laid schemes o mice and men*
> *Gang aft agley*,*   * often go wrong
> *An' lea'e us nought but grief an pain,*
> *For promis'd joy.*

On man's frailties Burns's thoughts ran deep, but he expressed them in language both beautiful and simple . . .

> *He heart ay's the part ay'*
> *That makes us right or wrang.*

Robert Burns brought common decency into life where there had been very little before. He raised hope where it had been dashed by the world around. He taught self respect where there was little encouragement for such a virtue. And as if that were not enough, he rescued the Scottish tongue at a time when strong forces were anglicising it, and he gave the Scottish people back their sense of nationhood at the moment when the country was fast becoming mere North Britain, an appendage of England. Had Burns not paved the way, Walter Scott could not have helped the Scots to re-discover the traditions and beauty of their homeland.

But Burns is probably best remembered for his songs - over 300 of them, expressing every emotion from loyalty to love, and for every occasion from meeting to parting. Burns's songs live on, but it is *Auld*

Lang Syne, that song most closely associated with meeting and parting, which had become an essential part, not just of every Burns Supper, but of any gathering of Scots. *Auld Lang Syne* is an international song of brotherhood and has been translated into many languages. To Scots it takes on deep meaning, reminding them of times that are gone and of places which have meant much to them in the past - as we sing it each of us remembers our own braes and our own burns, but we do not feel sad because *Auld Lang Syne* is not a sad song. It ends on an upbeat note of happiness and hope, offering the hand of friendship and promise of future meeting . . .

> *And there's a hand my trusty fiere!**   * companion
> *And gie's a hand o thine!*
> *And we'll tak a right gude-willy Waught,*
> *For auld land syne.*

No wonder *Auld Lang Syne* is an essential part of each and every Burns gathering. For it alone Burns deserves immortality - but he gave us more, much, much more.

With such humanity bonded to poetic skill it is hardly surprising that people quickly realised that his death had robbed them of a friend as well as an inspiration, and in response to that deep feeling the Burns cult grew spontaneously

1800 The first biography of Robert Burns appeared in this year, only four years after his death. It was written by James Currie, a Dumfriesshire-born man who was a doctor in Liverpool. Currie's biography has been much criticised because it contained inaccuracies and was critical of the Poet's way of life, especially his drinking habits. There is much to criticise in Currie's work, but in the doctor's favour it must be said that no one else would write the book, and he put it together hastily in order to raise money to help Jean and her family, and this it certainly did.

1801 The first meeting of Burns enthusiasts took place at Alloway, and the first Burns club was formed Greenock, Greenock Burns Club is now known within the Burns movement as the Mother Club.

1802 The first Burns Suppers were held at Alloway and Greenock.

1805 Paisley Burns Club, now called the Daughter Club, was inaugurated, with Robert Tannahill, the poet, as its first secretary.

1815 A fine mausoleum was erected in Dumfries and the Poet's body was re-interred there together with those of his sons, Maxwell and Francis Wallace. Jean was interred here in due course after her death in 1834.

1823 Burns Monument was built at Alloway.

1834 Jean Armour Burns, the poet's widow, died in Dumfries.

1844 Thousands of people, including Burns's sons and sister, marched to Alloway in pouring rain, and at the cottage doffed their hats to the Poet. This was followed by a luncheon for a thousand people with no haggis, but with what the Editor of *Punch* described as 'a piece of cold tongue, a plate of gooseberries almost ripe, and a pint of some mystery calling itself sherry.'

1859 The centenary of the Poet's birth brought a great resurgence of interest in Burns all round the English-speaking world. Practically every town in England had its own celebration, but the centrepiece was a gathering of 15,000 people at the Crystal Palace in London to hear speeches, music and the winning poem in a competition which had attracted over 600 entries. In Scotland there were processions, dinners and concerts by the score. A triumphal arch was erected in Dumfries and at Ayr a long procession marched to the Auld Kirk for divine service before making its way to Alloway. Shops closed for the day in many Scottish towns, although in Aberdeen, where folk are cannier, they shut only for the afternoon. The Poet's son told his audience that his father had once remarked to his mother, 'Jean, one hundred years hence they'll think mair o' me than they do now'. He was right: by 1859 Burns's enemies were all dead, and the new generation of Scots would not hear a word against him.

1885 The Burns movement became more organised under the newly formed Burns Federation.

1896 The centenary of Burns's death brought more celebrations round the world. That year the Henley-Henderson edition of his poetry added a new degree of scholarship to his work. That same year a statue of Highland Mary was unveiled at Dunoon - although no statue of Jean has ever been erected.

1959 The bi-centenary of the Poet's birth brought many events to Ayrshire with special dinners, a play about Burns, a pageant and a royal visit to Alloway.

1996 To mark the bi-centenary of Burns's death festivities were held by clubs around the world and a special concert in Glasgow, but the event that touched most hearts was a ploughing match at Mossgiel in the very field where the Poet turned over the mouse's nest. Nineteen pairs of horses competed and the event, expected to attract a few hundred spectators, brought 10,000 people to watch.

As the Burns movement grows stronger, one feature remains stable - the Burns Supper. It is impossible to say how many of these take place each January, for those organised by clubs within the Federation are only a tip of a very large iceberg. Scores are held in towns and villages, sponsored by local groups, women's organisations, churches and leisure clubs. Needless to say, the range in quality is considerable, but Robert Burns would not complain about that. He would hate the idea of a 'standard' Burns Supper, and would expect the whole evening to be one of 'noise and clatter', which is how a Burns Night ought to go.

And yet, as Scots we want to show the world what a great man our very own poet Robert Burns was. As a result, as the Editor of Punch pointed out, we do tend to be earnest in expressing our gratitude and our penitence. You should be grateful and penitent on 25 January by all means, but combine the haggis and whisky with good speeches and good crack, and send your guests home wanting to read more of his verse and follow the good advice that it contains. Robert Burns himself would ask for no more.

Have a happy and successful Burns Night.

COULD I REALLY RUN
A BURNS SUPPER?

Of course you could - but if you can persuade someone else to do it instead, don't! At most Anniversary Dinners there's plenty of sympathy for the young singer who is showing nerves, or for the speaker whose worried look tells that he is willing the last trump to sound before the time comes to stand up and propose his toast. But not a thought is spared for the person who has spent up to a year arranging every detail of the evening so carefully that it all passes without a hitch, and without anyone noticing that it was organised at all. It looks as if it just happened!

No, that is not quite true: at the end of the evening there should be a vote of thanks to the organiser or organisers, who have taken so much trouble to make it go well. And Burnsians are kind folk so, even if one or two problems have arisen, these will be forgotten and the arranger will still receive warm thanks.

That does not mean that the organiser can sit back and relax when grace is said. He - or she - will be the only person who doesn't enjoy the haggis because they are too busy trying to catch the head waiter's eye to make sure he has brought dressing for a vegetarian top table guest's salad (although it should be pointed out that vegetarian haggis is available, and very good it is too!) He (or she) may be the only person at table who doesn't hear a word of the *Address to the Unco Guid*, or a note of *Ae Fond Kiss* because he is transfixed by a gimlet-eyed guest who thinks he hasn't been allocated as good a place at table as he believes he deserves. The organiser is the one person who staggers home exhausted.

If the dinner is organised on behalf of a Burns Club or other society, the secretary usually has the task of making all the arrangements, However, a smart secretary delegates, and makes sure that all the work does not rest on his shoulders. And that's only fair.

COULD I REALLY RUN A BURNS SUPPER?

Arranging a Burns Anniversary Dinner is really too big a task to impose on one person, and most larger clubs appreciate this and set up a sub-committee to share the work, but smaller clubs and organisation who hold a Burns Supper as part of a full social programme, tend to leave the organisation to the secretary, or at most to two or three people.

If you are asked to take on the job of arranging the event, especially if you have never done it before, ask for a small sub-committee to help you. This means that you will have wider experience than your own to call upon, and on the night, there will be others to take care of such details as the table plan, general guests' needs, meal arrangements and entertainers, while you devote yourself to the top table guests and overall arrangements.

Fortunately the Burns movement is a close and friendly one, so wherever you are, there will be a pool of deep knowledge of Burns anniversary dinners available to guide you. So don't hesitate to ask for help - every Burns Supper organiser has to start somewhere, and all of us have enough memories of our own near-disasters during those early days to understand and show you sympathy. Even if you don't belong to a Burns Club, contact the Secretary or Chairman of your local one for guidance on procedure or help to find speakers. And if you are unable to solve your problem through the local club, then get in touch with the Robert Burns World Federation (formerly known as the Burns Federation) headquarters at the Dick Institute in Kilmarnock and seek their help. The Federation exists to ensure that Robert Burns's memory is well served, and they will do their utmost to ensure that yours maintains the high standard they demand from member clubs.

Organising a Burns Supper, even with the help of a committee, is not easy, but it is rewarding when guests tell you at the end what a wonderful evening they have spent. Better still is to hear that through the Burns Club grapevine, and to find that every other club for miles around is after your speakers for their next year's dinner . .

If you feel equal to this rewarding task, read on.

Don't think too hard about where to start planning the event - just plunge in like a swimmer bound for the other side of the English Channel and keep going. Or you can sit down with pencil and paper and draw up a list of what has to be done, and more important, when it has to be done. The second method is by far the best.

But where to start planning the Anniversary Dinner is not half as important as when to start. If you are reading this on 26 January, then it is not a minute too soon to begin work on next year's dinner - after all Burns Night is a mere 364 days away, unless this is a leap year, in which case you have an extra 24 hours. Yippee, that should be a big help!

Here is how your list might look.
At each step, write in the details of what has been arranged:

┌─────────────────── ACTION LIST ───────────────────┐

Venue ....

....

Telephone ....
Menu ....

....

....

....

....

....

Printer ....
Speeches ....

....

....

....

....

....

Entertainment ....

....

....

....

Costing ....

....

....

Check in January ....

....

....

The Night ....
Your name and address* ....

....

....

└──┘

* As it is vital not to lose details of arrangements, be sure to add your own name
and address at the bottom of it.
The above "Action List" could be photocopied for your own use.

THE DATE

Deciding on the most suitable date for your Burns Supper is the first thing to be settled, but before discussing it with others in your organising group, check dates of other anniversary dinners or competing events in your area. This is not as difficult as it sounds, for one local Burns Club secretary will probably be able to supply the dates of all major events planned in the district for the following year.

Many clubs have a set date to which they adhere year by year, often avoiding 25 January itself because on that night other important Suppers are held. Instead they choose another date close to the anniversary and adhere to it from year to year - say, 26 January, or the Friday preceding the 25th. Some even hold their dinner fortnight earlier than Burns Night, so that they can have a better choice of speakers and local dignitaries, and newspapers will be more likely to have a reporter free to attend.

Decide on an evening which suits you, but earmark an alternative before you go any further just in case problems arise with venue or speakers.

THE VENUE

Like the best Burns speakers and entertainers, the most suitable places to hold Burns Suppers are often booked a full year or more ahead. It is quite usual for a secretary, before he leaves at the end of a dinner, to ask the manager to pencil in a date for next year's event. And a good rule of thumb is that the better the place, the further ahead you need to book. With the date chosen, decide roughly how many people will be likely to attend, how much space you will need (especially if a dance display is to be included in the entertainment programme), and how elaborate a menu you want. Then it is time to get down to making detailed arrangements. Make a file to hold notes of all meetings with caterers to discuss arrangements and keep copies of all letters sent out or received in connection with the event. Near the date of the dinner you should keep this file close to the telephone so that you can refer to the relevant papers when people ring up with problems, or to discuss details. The organised organiser is always several moves ahead of the one who just jots down notes on the back of an old envelope and pushes it into his inside jacket pocket!

With this file you will look as if you mean business as you visit suitable hotels, restaurants and banqueting suites, or talk to caterers. Neither drop in casually to a potential venue or caterer, nor make your arrangements verbally as your leave after dining there one evening - the club secretary who makes a provisional booking for the following year at the end of the dinner will certainly confirm it in writing within a few days. And never, never make your arrangements by telephone. Arrange an appointment in advance and set aside time to discuss everything in detail. If the manager (or banqueting manager) gives the impression than he cannot spare the time to talk to you now, then the chances are that you will see very little of him on The Night. In the same way, if you rush into his office and out again, he will feel that you are not bringing to his establishment a prestigious function which will make him the envy of every other caterer in the town.

Tell him everything - explain what sort of Anniversary Dinner it is to be (formal, with very important speakers and probably Burns Federation representatives present, or a friendly informal club get-together). Give details of your speakers and entertainers, and of the sort of meal you are looking for. The more he knows, the more exactly he can tailor his services to your needs.

Ask to see the room, reception facilities for the principal guests, pre-dinner bar facilities, car parking area - the lot. Make sure that the room is large enough to allow top table guests to walk in procession to table, and that there is space for the haggis ceremony. A Burns Supper is not like any other dinner: the entertainment lasts a long time and guests have to be able to set their chairs back an inch or two and relax while they enjoy it. If a room can take 100 diners for a formal dinner, then 80 will be enough for a Burns Night celebration.

MENU

At the outset I must confess I prefer to call the Burns Night menu the Bill of Fare since that is what Burns called it in his *Address to the Haggis*.

> *Ye Pow'rs, wha mak mankind your care,*
> *   And dish them out their **bill o fare**,*
> *Auld Scotland wants nae skinking ware*
> *   That jaups in luggies:*

Most catering establishments worthy of the name have plenty of experience in catering for Burns Suppers, and certainly there are advantages in going to one which is practised in the art of honouring the Poet. Besides, it saves a lot of explaining how you want everything done!

The venue ought to have standard Burns Night bills of fare to show you, with haggis as the focal point of them, but you will have to decide whether it is to be the main course or simply a subsidiary one. It is good to see haggis as the principal dish of the evening, but I confess that this view can be tempered by attending three Burns Suppers on successive nights! People may prefer something less rich as the main course, so it is a good idea to test the opinion of a few fellow members of your organisation in advance on this question.

Apart from haggis you can serve whatever you think your guests will enjoy. Soup is popular as the first course and it is an appropriate part of the traditional Scottish farm kitchen. Cock-a-Leekie (chicken and leek soup), Scotch Broth (barley broth) or Bawd Bree (hare soup) are the most popular. This is the one meal of the year in which soup should be plain and home-made.

If haggis is to be the main course then a fish dish, probably salmon, can be served to follow. Herring would be more appropriate, but it is difficult to get a caterer to serve it these days. Many clubs have their own traditions as at Alloa where the Burns Club, which began life as Alloa Tripe Club, serves tripe and onions instead of fish.

Then follows the Haggis, highlight of the meal, with all the usual ceremonial (see pages 46-50) and served with champit tatties (mashed potatoes) and bashed neeps (mashed turnip: in England it's called swede). The potato and turnip sometimes are mashed together with seasoning and butter to form a traditional Orkney dish called Clapshaw. It is a great pity that this is not more often served at home in Scotland nowadays for it is a delicious way of serving the vegetables. The two vegetables combine to form a delicately tasting, rich accompaniment to meat, which is quite different from the individual taste of each. Try Clapshaw at home once and you will never want to eat the two separately again.

If the haggis is not to be the main course, the choice to follow is often Roastit Beef or Roastit Bubblyjock (turkey) with all the trimmings. Turkey is a very popular choice today. If you expect vegetarian guests, you should provide a suitable dish for them - even if it is vegetarian haggis!

In times past dessert was usually such traditional dishes as Hattit Kit (a kind of curded milk) or Apple Frushie (apple tart), but nowadays anything goes, from Peach Melba to Coupe Jacques. Perhaps the most popular dessert is Sherry Trifle, served under a variety of names from Scotch Trifle to Tipsy Laird.

To round off the meal, bannocks or oatcakes follow, served with a kebbuck of cheese - preferably Dunlop Cheese from Ayrshire - or Crowdie (a cream cheese). If the area in which you live has its own special cheese, serve that by all means: Burns would approve! Although the evening is long it is a pity to rush such a meal, so it is always wise to start early and take time to enjoy these traditional dishes which are as much part of Burns Night as the speeches, recitations and songs. Sometimes several of the speeches, recitations, or songs are interspersed between courses.

THE PRINTER

Invitations, bill of fare and the toast lists are usually printed, unless the celebration is to be a very informal one at which costs have to be kept to a minimum. With word processors easily available nowadays, it is easy to produce printed matter with a professional look cheaply. There are two points to take into consideration, however - a well printed bill of fare on the table enhances the enjoyment at the time and will be retained afterwards as a memento of a happy evening, so before deciding to "do it yourself", obtain estimates from printers. You may be surprised to discover how little more it costs to have them professionally printed. Be sure to get written quotations for each item as you go along, however.

Costs can be cut, by avoiding use of illustrations, tartan ribbons or colour printing on the bill of fare, or gilt edges on the invitation card, but here again, do remember you are presenting each guest with what will be a memento of the occasion. If cost is an essential consideration, a simple white card, well printed in blue to suggest the colours of the Saltire, will provide a perfectly acceptable Scottish effect, and will look really good and give status to the occasion.

Always obtain estimates from at least two printers for all print work and ask in advance if printing a small run of, say, 75 menu cards is the kind of work in which they specialise. It is no good going to a firm which is geared to supplying half a million leaflets to a Government Department and expecting it to compete with a small man who does bills and invitations for local societies all the year round.

Ask secretaries of other societies to recommend names of suitable printers, then go along and discuss your print requirements and ask for estimates in writing.

You will need several printed items:

Invitations: If it's a club dinner, invitations to the principal guests, local dignitaries, press, and other invitees must be sent out in good time, and they must look smart enough to do you credit. Have them printed as elegantly as possible on good quality card, to make your guests feel important and look forward to the evening, Post them by the end of October at the latest.

Tickets to be sold should also look tempting and prestigious enough to be displayed proudly on their mantelpiece - you never know, that might tempt other people to want to come along. Print the ticket in the most attractive manner you can afford.

Receipts. Remember to cost in the price of receipts if these have to be sent to people who apply for tickets.

Bill of fare The bill of fare will double as a programme for the evening's entertainment, and here again, don't stint on quality.

Wording depends on how formal you wish the dinner to be, but your printer will guide you on the most appropriate way of putting it. A typical bill of fare can be found on page 31.

THE SPEECHES

Two toasts, the Immortal Memory and the toast to the Lassies, are obligatory: others are optional at the discretion of the organisers, and can be to the club or society, to brother clubs, to the town or district, to Scotland, or (in the case of dinners outside Scotland) the host country. An appreciation of the Immortal Memory should also be given. These speeches are discussed later, so the main points for your list are to choose the speakers with care, and invite them early. Good speakers are often booked up for years ahead. At many Burns Club events the proposer of the Immortal Memory is the Chairman's personal guest and is chosen by him.

The haggis ceremony is not a speech, but it is a key part of the dinner, and for it you will need a piper to pipe it in, and a member of your organisation or invited guest to recite *The Address to the Haggis*. Be sure to remember both on your list.

THE ENTERTAINMENT

How long the sangs and clatter should last after the dinner is over, depends entirely upon the stamina of your guests, but one piece of good advice is not to make it overlong. It is a good idea to intersperse the courses of the dinner with a song, recitation, or airs to songs played on the violin or piano. Here anything goes - choose whichever poems and songs you wish.

However, *Tam o' Shanter* is (almost) compulsory! No Burns Supper feels complete without it, and from my experience there seem to be a lot of men around Scotland who specialise in reciting this epic adventure of the Carrick farmer's encounter with the witches at the old ruined kirk at Alloway on the way home after a heavy evening's drinking. Do try to include it - recited from memory if possible, rather than read.

Choose a varied selection of poems and songs, which will reflect the immense range of the Bard's skill and genius, and find singers and readers or reciters who can do these justice. These performers hold the key to a memorable evening with Burns, so choose your performers carefully, book them early - not forgetting an accompanist - and check what fees and travel costs will be involved.

COSTING IT OUT

The meal, other venue costs, piper's and entertainers' fees or travel costs, printer's bill, postages, telephone charges, and all other expected expenses should be totalled, remembering to add on VAT or service charges. It is important to get this right, so check and re-check to make sure. Then add on a small margin, of up to ten percent, for those unexpected extras which will almost certainly crop up, and you will have a fair idea of the global cost of the evening. Divide this total by the number of tickets you expect to sell and you have the price to be charged for tickets. Always remember that the difference between profit and loss in organising this kind of event is narrow; it is also the margin between your peace of mind and worry, so run over all the costs again, and ask a fellow club member to check them before settling on the ticket price. If you must err, do so on the side of caution, so that you will not be faced with a loss. Any profit can be given to a charity, preferably one with a Burns connection, and here the Robert Burns World Federation will help you to find one.

CHECK IN JANUARY

At the beginning of January go through every detail on your list. Contact the venue manager, speakers, piper and artistes to reminded of their commitments. It may sound foolish to suggest that the man who is to propose the Immortal Memory may forget or have double booked, but it can happen. Popular speakers are trysted years ahead - often over the table at some other dinner or at a chance meeting in the street - and it is easy for them to forget to put it into their diary later. By all means seize the opportunity to book someone when you meet informally, but follow the invitation up by letter at once, keeping a copy for your file. During the month leading up to the Supper there will probably be calls from the venue, to check details - note, they have their action list too! And you will almost certainly be contacted by guests who have to cancel due to illness or for personal reasons as well as by others asking if tickets are still available. With luck these will balance out. Also expect a host of special requests to be seated beside friends, or for someone who is a bit hard of hearing to be given a place near the top table and so on. However trivial or unimportant these requests may sound in relation to your enormous task of organising the evening, they are important to the person making them and should be dealt with sympathetically. People feel strongly about Burns, and they feel equally strongly about Burns Suppers; many a storm has blown up, and friendship foundered because of a demand for special treatment at a Burns Supper which could not be met. Solomon and Job together could not produce a solution acceptable to some people, and it is foolish to try - better be firm at the start and say the request cannot be met than to build up hopes only to dash them later. With nothing left to chance you are ready for The Great Night.

THE BIG NIGHT

Time has flown since that day, probably the best part of a year ago, when the first inspection was made of the venue and it was decided to hold your Burns Supper there. Tickets have sold well, principal guests have all confirmed that they will be present, and programmes have arrived from the printers, been checked and found to in perfect order.

That's a relief, especially as the last few days will have brought telephone calls from the venue to check details.

THE SEATING PLAN

One way or another the seating plan will give a headache for days, and may well not be settled satisfactorily until every member of the company has taken his or her place at the table. Some clubs never allocate places, but let it be first come first served. In such cases guests arrive an hour or more before the dinner and when the doors are opened make an undignified scramble for places near the speakers. Even then there are complaints of seats being taken unfairly, or of scarves and bags placed on chairs to reserve places, being switched.

My own preference is for a table plan to be prepared in advance with seats allocated so that guests and committee members are interspersed among the other members. Even better is to have place names at every seat, so that everybody knows where they are to sit. Musicians and singers should be at tables near the piano so that they can be in position quickly when called upon to perform.

Whichever method is adopted, the organiser needs an efficient band of helpers to cope with seating problems at the start of the function. He will have plenty other things on his mind at that time without having to worry about the fact that old Mr. MacGregor's hearing-aid battery is flat so he needs a place under the nose of the principal speaker.

LAST MINUTE JOBS

This is a long day for the organiser; final adjustments will have to be made to the seating plan and the actual plan typed out ready to be pinned on a board at the entrance or in the room where the reception is being held. Another plan in the VIP reception room is a sound idea; that way the main guests will know what acquaintances are to be present. Throughout the morning of the dinner the organiser will have to deal with telephone queries, then he will want to visit the venue to make a last inspection and deliver programmes, table-plans and other literature or display material for the evening. He will be back at the venue in good time to give his Chairman a final briefing, to allocate jobs to other officials and to be ready to receive the guests, looking as if he hadn't a care in the world.

TOP TABLE PLAN

It will have been decided well in advance who sits at the top table. There are no hard and fast rules about numbers or positions, except that the principal speaker will be on the right of the Chairman, in the place of honour. Also at the Chairman's table will be the other speakers, representatives of the Burns Federation, the clergyman who is to say grace, the local civic leader, and any other special guest the Chairman has chosen

to invite. Husbands or wives of these guests should also be included in the top table party.

A special room is usually set aside for the Chairman and his guests, and they have their pre-dinner drinks there while the club members and their guests are gathering in the main room. When everybody is seated at table the top table party will enter the dining room in procession, led by a piper. It is the organiser's job to arrange this procession in the order in which they will sit, starting with the person at the end of the table on the left of the Chairman. At a signal the company will stand and the Chairman and his guests enter and walk round the room clockwise to their places, usually to handclaps from the waiting company. If the layout of the room is such that the top table party have to march in anticlockwise then the order will be reversed and start with the person who is to sit at the right-hand end of the table.

When the Chairman and principal guests have taken their places, the organiser can relax - in theory at least. If he has done his preparatory work well and has a band of efficient helpers round him all should have gone smoothly so far.

THE CHAIRMAN

The Chairman takes charge of the proceedings the moment he reaches his place at table, and from then on the success of the evening becomes largely his responsibility. It is his duty to ensure that speeches, songs and music move along briskly, but also with dignity and humour so that everyone goes home, as they ought to after a Burns Supper, feeling better folk.

Of course there must be fun at a Burns Supper - Burns would have insisted on it - but there must also be a serious element as well, especially in the Immortal Memory, which has not only to honour the Poet but must inspire the listeners to read Burns, to think about his achievement and as a result to improve their own lives. Burns is revered by Scots; he deserves that love and respect, and the Immortal Memory must give him what is due to him.

If you are Chairman you carry responsibility for this.

You also must put the whole company at ease from the start by showing that you yourself are at ease. Be neither indifferent nor diffident in your opening remarks, and a story, preferably with relevance to the club or group present is an excellent aid to this; then having put your stamp on the evening at this early stage, you must maintain the tone as you introduce each speaker or performer.

You carry responsibility for the actual mechanics of the celebrations - when to serve each course of the meal and when to introduce each speaker or performer. Make sure you are seated within sight of the secretary so that you can give a signal if anything is not going according to plan or if someone needs a reminder to do his allotted task.

The waiting staff have a job to do serving and clearing courses and serving refreshments, but not during the speeches and entertainment. Burns Suppers and other events have been ruined by waiters doing their work - they may think quietly - during speeches or songs. It's your job to see that this doesn't happen. At the same time you must give the serving staff time and opportunity to do their job. A short pause between items will allow for this, but the staff must be instructed in advance of the evening's programme, so the organiser will have seen to it that this has been done.

If you are chairing the Burns Supper the chances are that you are the current year's President of the Club, and so will have kept in close touch with the organiser all the year round, helping and advising on every aspect, but especially where the speakers are concerned.

In many clubs the proposer of the Immortal Memory is the Chairman's guest - his personal choice of speaker - although he usually consults the committee to make sure that he has secured the very best talent available. In other clubs the whole committee pools its knowledge of speakers and takes a vote to decide which shall be chosen. The secretary will then write to invite him to speak, but the Chairman (probably accompanied by one or two committee members) will brief him nearer the time of the dinner on what the club expects of him and what the "tone" of the evening will be.

Burns Suppers come in many degrees of what *Punch* at the Festival of 1844 called "earnestness", and the Chairman will see that on The Night the right degree of earnestness is maintained. Because he is President of the Club the Chairman will be a long-standing and respected member, well aware of the organisation's aims and aspirations. He may have served as Vice-President and, in that office, will have helped and advised the previous Chairman. The vice-presidency can be regarded as a rehearsal for this evening, this crowning event of his presidential year.

During his vice-presidency the Chairman will have learnt much that will give him confidence tonight, but he will be nervous just like all the other "performers". He must be serious most of the time, but not solemn. A joke or two will thaw the company, but that does not mean he should try to be a fast-talking comedian. There is nothing more painful to an audience than listening to an unfunny person trying to be funny. Every man knows in his own heart where he stands as a teller of funny stories, so it is up to him to tailor what he says to his own personality. Do not rely on others to tell you how well your jokes have gone down - you can sense the reaction of the audience and get a more honest answer from inside your own head.

Do you need notes? Again, only you know whether you are likely to forget vital points or even to dry up if you don't have something in writing to remind you. For me notes are the key to getting everything right on The Night; but they should not be so full that they are read off the paper. Only a competent actor could deliver such a script convincingly. A few key points are really all that is needed as an *aide memoire*.

Quotations are a different matter. The most practised of speakers can dry up in the middle of a poem - even one he knows - to the intense embarrassment of himself and his audience. It is a good idea to have quotations written out on a small piece of paper so that they can be consulted unobtrusively if necessary. Be certain that any quotations you intend to use are not a vital part of what a guest speaker has to say - you could so easily ruin his speech by using his key quotation first. So tell the speaker which Burns quotes you intend to use.

It is always useful to have a full programme in front of you giving names of songs, poems and performers, although these are printed on the bill of fare or programme for the evening. If they have not been printed, type them out on a sheet of paper and let this lie on the table so that you can work down the list item by item, without fear of omitting anything or anyone.

Check carefully the background of every speaker and performer so that they can be introduced in a proper way and no relevant detail will be forgotten. If he has written a book on Burns, mention it, if he is noted locally as a pigeon fancier, refer to that. It is only courteous to give his background, especially highlighting any point which links him with Burns. If that seems too obvious a point, let me merely say that I have been introduced by Chairmen who have gone into all the detail about my early life and career - all past history - and omitted to say what I do at the present day and that I have written books on Burns.

Getting details of the background of your speakers or performers wrong is as bad as getting their names wrong. It is important to them that they should be correctly presented to the gathering, so be courteous enough to ensure that their introduction brings out aspects of their background which are not only relevant but the ones they would like presented.

The Chairman's first job is to welcome the company, which should be done in a few short friendly sentences. There is no need to go into detail about the speakers at this stage - merely to extend a welcome to them, to other important guests and to the assembled company generally, wishing them all a happy evening of companionship through Robert Burns, who himself liked nothing better than to be among friends, enjoying good food, a dram and companionship.

THE GRACE

Grace starts the meal, and if the club has an honorary padre or a clergyman present, that can be delegated to him: otherwise the Chairman will say grace.

The usual and most appropriate grace for tonight is the Selkirk Grace, which is regarded as the Poet's own special one, although it has little connection with him or with the Border town of Selkirk for that matter.

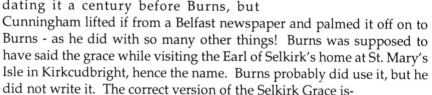

The Selkirk Grace was first attributed to Burns by Allan Cunningham in his 1834 life and works of Burns. I have seen this grace referred to as The Covenanter's Grace, dating it a century before Burns, but Cunningham lifted if from a Belfast newspaper and palmed it off on to Burns - as he did with so many other things! Burns was supposed to have said the grace while visiting the Earl of Selkirk's home at St. Mary's Isle in Kirkcudbright, hence the name. Burns probably did use it, but he did not write it. The correct version of the Selkirk Grace is-

> *Some have meat and cannot eat,*
> *Some can not eat that want it:*
> *But we have meat and we can eat*
> *Sae let the Lord be thankit*

It is more common to render the Grace in its earlier wholly-Scottish version, and in the light of its tenuous Burns connection this seems fair enough:

Some hae meat and canna eat,
And some wad eat that want it:
But we hae meat and we can eat
And sae the Lord be thankit.

The first course of the dinner is now served, enjoyed and cleared, and the Chairman rises to welcome the haggis.

THE HAGGIS

The Haggis forms the central part of the Bill of Fare and, apart from the Immortal Memory, is the focus of the evening because this is a dish which takes every Scot back to the manner in which they imagine people lived in Burns's time, although in truth, few farm folk in Ayrshire saw much meat - even haggis - in those days. Nevertheless, alongside oatmeal, haggis links our generation to that of our forefathers who made Scotland what she is today.

The haggis is a lordly dish of excellent pedigree, but it is myth to say it was given to us by the French and derives its name from the French word hachis, meaning minced meat. If the haggis was a culinary gift of the Auld Alliance between France and Scotland it is much more likely that it was the Scots who gave it to the French rather than the other way round.

F. Marian McNeill, in her classic work, The Scots Kitchen, points out that the name haggis is more likely to be derived from the old Scottish word hag which means to hack or to chop.

Food historian and cookery expert, Clarissa Dickson Wright, in her gloriously entertaining and informative book The Haggis: a Little History, agrees, and adds that she has seen no dish that resembles haggis in the well-documented culinary history of France. However, "dishes made in the maw of an animal are still found in Scandinavia,", she writes, "and haggis is eaten with relish by Scandinavian visitors to Scotland, who frequently remark on its similarity to some dish in their own local cuisine." The Vikings who arrived first as seasonal raiders soon became permanent settlers and the northern isles did not become part of Scotland until 1468. "Whether or not the Vikings took haggis with them on their raiding voyages will never be known," she says. "But they undoubtedly took their sheep - or other people's - when they settled, and their womenfolk took their traditional skills and recipes."

Marion McNeill describes the dish, relating it to Burns. "The haggis is in fact simply a superior sausage, or, as Burns describes it, the 'great chieftain o' the puddin (sausage) race', and like the sausage it was once common to many lands. Of course the contents must have varied as much as do those of the sausage in our own time. To such as still 'look down wi sneerin', scornfu' view on sic a dinner', we would point out that the most aesthetic of nations, the ancient Greeks, had a haggis of their own, which was immortalised by Aristophanes in The Clouds".

The haggis of Burns's day and as we know it today, is a tribute to the Scottish gift of making something of excellence out of cheap materials. Its ingredients are heart, lights and liver, beef suet, oatmeal and onions minced together and sewn into the large stomach bag of a sheep.

The perfect haggis is neither so dry that it crumbles like cake, nor so wet that it clings to fork and plate and then to the palate. Haggis-makers who can get the blend right spend busy weeks in January to satisfy the demand which comes to them from every quarter.

Alas, haggis is almost never made at home nowadays, even in Scotland, which is a pity for one of the most memorable dishes I ever ate as a child was a haggis which my mother made according to an old recipe. As I remember it, mother's haggis was rather like a mealy pudding, but not over spicy, and had a slight sweetness to it. It was enormous and seemed to last for days, eaten first in the traditional way with potatoes and turnip (swede to the English), and then sliced cold and fried or toasted in front of the old kitchen range.

It was an experience to eat; a memory to be treasured. Never since have I tasted haggis like it, and the great pity is that I remember her making it only once.

Here is Marian McNeill's recipe for a traditional haggis. The ingredients are - the large stomach bag of a sheep, the pluck (including heart, lights and liver), beef-suet, pinhead (coarse) oatmeal, onions, black pepper, salt, stock or gravy.

This is her method:

THE HAGGIS

"Brown and birstle (dry or toast) a breakfast cupful of oatmeal before the fire or in the oven. Clean the great bag thoroughly, washing it first in cold water and then, after turning it inside out, scalding and scraping it with a knife; the let it soak overnight in cold salted water. In the morning put it aside with the rough side turned out. Wash the pluck well and put on to boil covered with cold water, letting the windpipe hang over the side of the pot to let out any impurities*. Let it boil for an hour and a half, then take it out and cut away the pipes and any superfluities of gristle. Mince the heart and lights and grate half the liver. (The rest of the liver is not required.) Put the minced and grated meat into a basin with half a pound of minced suet, two medium-sized onions finely chopped, and the toasted oatmeal, and season highly with black pepper and salt. (A pinch of cayenne say some housewives, 'makes all the difference'.) Over the whole pour, preferably when cold, as much of the liquid in which the pluck was boiled (or better still, good stock) as will make the mixture sappy. Fill the stomach bag rather more than half full - say five-eighths - as it requires plenty of room to swell. Sew it up securely and place it on an enamel plate in a pot of boiling water (to which half a pint of milk is often added), or, better still, boil it in stock. As soon as it begins to swell, prick it all over with a large needle to prevent its bursting. Boil steadily, without the lid, for three hours, adding boiling water as required to keep the haggis covered. Serve very hot without any garnish".

Nobody takes all that trouble today - there is no need to - because a number of butchers around Scotland still produce their own haggis. But undoubtedly the king of Scotland's haggis-makers is John Macsween, who has turned the manufacture of haggis into an art. Starting originally from his own butcher's shop in Bruntsfield in Edinburgh, he now produces many tons of 'the beastie' in a state of the art factory just outside the city. Macsween haggis forms the centrepiece of Burns Suppers (and other Scottish celebrations at other times of the year) for today it is being eaten more and more at St Andrews Night, Hogmanay, and even regularly as a meal at home. Macsween has turned the humble dish that was Burns's favourite dinner into a gourmet experience, with Macsween haggis sold in the grand shops of London and Edinburgh as well as in modest butchers' and delicatessens all over Britain. To keep abreast of modern demands John is constantly experimenting, and has even evolved a hugely

*Nowadays the wind-pipe is always removed.

successful vegetarian haggis. What Robert Burns would have thought of that is left unsaid, but a growing number of customers award it high praise! Thanks to John Macsween the haggis is now a lordly dish more widely enjoyed than ever it was.

The usual accompaniments are mashed potatoes and mashed turnip (swede) - tatties and neeps - or, better still, the two mashed together with pepper and a good piece of dripping as the delicious Orkney dish, Clapshaw.

To enjoy haggis to the full it should be eaten slowly and savoured. This is why I like to see it as the main course of the evening, rather than a mere entertainment between two other courses. Even if the haggis is not to be the main course, its presentation, service and enjoyment should not be skimped - Give the company long enough to admire it, to think about it, to savour it, and to reflect on what they have lost by letting it disappear from the daily menu.

Everybody enjoys the ritual presentation of the haggis and the address to it at table on Burns Night, and this seldom varies.

THE HAGGIS CEREMONY

When the preceding course has been cleared and the signal comes from the kitchen, the Chairman will call on the company to stand to receive the haggis. The "beastie" is then carried in by the chef, held high for all to see, and preceded by a piper and followed by a third person ceremonially carrying a couple of bottles of whisky for the traditional

dram at the end of the ceremony. The haggis is placed before the Chairman who either addresses the haggis himself or calls upon the person who is to recite the poem *To a Haggis*. I have heard of the haggis being fiddled in instead of piped, and I have a sneaking feeling that Burns, who loved fiddle music, would have enjoyed that, but it is more usual for a piper to do the honours.

The poem may be read, but it sounds far, far better recited from memory. A knife, the other most forgotten item at a Burns Supper, should already lie on the table so that, at the line "An' cut you up wi' ready slight" the haggis bag can be slit open. It is better for the people to be seated during the recitation of *To a Haggis* to allow them to have a better view of the ceremony of cutting the haggis open.

How the haggis, innocent creature that it is, can be ill treated at this moment! After being welcomed like the returning prodigal it is sometimes fallen upon with such venom that the knife shoots clean through the silver flat on which it rests, and pins both to the table. If the plate is a china one, then it smashes into smithereens, and I have heard of at least one occasion when this resulted in a fierce altercation to decide who should pay for the plate! Others attack the haggis wildly and with eyes shut tightly, all but severing the hand that holds the plate. At the other end of the scale there are the diffident haggis addressers who slide the knife along the bag so gently that the dirk glances off and the haggis slips to the floor.

Cutting the haggis bag open appears easy, but it is an art which comes only with practice. Remember the object of opening the bag is to reach the meat inside, and not to stab the haggis to death or to produce an incision for some exploratory surgical operation, so a good plan is to make two incisions in the form of a St Andrews Cross so that the bag can be folded back and the inside spooned out.

When the poem ends the company will applaud and stand again to toast the haggis. Three glasses of whisky should have been placed quietly on the table, ready for the Chairman to offer a glass to both piper and chef and one for himself, and call for a toast to the haggis at the end of the ceremony. If whisky is not being served to all guests, those members of the company who like whisky with their haggis will have ordered their dram in time to join in this toast. All men who play the bagpipes have good strong lungs and the piper's voice will echo round the room as he calls out the traditional Gaelic Toast of "Slainte mhath" (your good health).

The chef and piper then leave and the haggis is served to all the guests.

Incidentally, the piper is one person whose invitation to play can be easily overlooked, and at Chesterfield, in Derbyshire, I'm told the Burns Club has solved that problem neatly by making the piper an honorary life member.

There is no need to down the whisky at a draught: after the toast it can be savoured slowly as the haggis is served. But please don't pour it over the haggis - that spoils the taste of good haggis and ruins excellent whisky. I have suggested some other drinks that go well with haggis later. (see page 101)

Here is the poem for you to memorise:

TO A HAGGIS

Fair fa' your honest, sonsie* face,   *plump
    Great Chieftain o' the Puddin-race!
Aboon them a' ye tak your place,
    Painch, tripe or thairm:*   *intestine
Weel are ye wordy of a grace
    As lang's my arm.

The groaning trencher there ye fill,
    Your hurdies* like a distant hill,   *buttocks
Your pin wad help to mend a mill
    In time o' need
While thro' your pores the dews distil
    Like amber bead.

His knife see Rustic-labour dight,*   *wipe
    An' cut you up wi' ready slight,
Trenching your gushing entrails bright
    Like onie ditch;
And then, O what a glorious sight,
    Warm, reekin, rich!

Then, horn for horn they stretch an' strive,
    Deil tak the hindmost, on they drive,
Till a' their weel-swall'd kytes belyve*   *quickly
    Are bent like drums;
Then auld Guidman, maist like to rise,
    Be thankit hums.

Is there that owre his French ragout,
    Or olio wad staw* a sow,   *sicken
Or fricassee wad mak her spew
    Wi perfect scunner,*   *revulsion
Looks down wi' sneering, scornfu' view
    On sic a dinner?

Poor devil! see him owre his trash,
As feckless as a wither'd rash,
His spindle shank a guid whip-lash
His nieve* a nit*   *fist *nut
Thro' bluidy flood or field to dash,
O how unfit!

But mark the Rustic, haggis-fed,
The trembling earth resounds his tread,
Clap in his walie* nieve a blade,   *large
He'll mak' it whistle;
An' legs, an' arms, an' heads will sned,*   *be cut off
Like taps o' thristle.*   *thistle

Ye pow'rs wha mak mankind your care,
And dish them out their bill o' fare,
Auld Scotland wants nae skinking* ware   *watery
That jaups in luggies;*   *milk pails
But, if ye wish her gratefu' pray'r,
Gie her a Haggis!

With relief everybody can now settle down to enjoy the haggis, followed by roastit bubbly-jock and crowdie cheese, or whatever is on the bill of fare without a care until the last plate has been cleared.

INTERLUDE

Just as at any other function there will be some who will want to smoke as soon as the meal is over, and they will be waiting patiently for the Chairman to propose the Loyal Toast and grant permission to smoke as the coffee is being served.

Coffee and the interval before the speeches form an interlude during which guests, officials and members of the company can relax before the serious business of paying tribute to the Bard begins. This is an opportune moment for messages of good wishes from other societies to be read, or for formal Club business announcements to be made. Tickets for other functions run by the Club can be sold and raffle tickets for Burns or other charities can be taken round.

The Burns World Federation certainly would be grateful at this time for a mention of its good work, and for copies of the annual *Burns Chronicle* to be sold. The *Chronicle* which provides an excellent introduction to Burns for anyone who is unfamiliar with the Poet or his writings contains articles reflecting deep research into lesser known aspects of his life and work and gives the non-Burnsian some indication of the dimension of good which the Federation provides for Scottish literature and the Scots way of life generally. Certainly the *Chronicle* contains enough thought-provoking material to fan the smallest spark of interest in Burns into a great fire of enthusiasm for the man and his achievement.

The Federation would also approve of a collection to contribute to its own ambitious schools competitions, or in aid of a Burns-linked charity such as the National Burns Memorial and Cottage Homes, or the Jean Armour Burns Houses at Mauchline. Alternatively, a collection might be made towards some broadly-based Scottish cultural charity like the Scottish National Dictionary to which the Federation has contributed much time and effort over many years.

The Scottish National Dictionary Association has published a 10-volume dictionary which is a record of the Scottish language, spoken and written, since 1700, followed by a one-volume Concise Scottish Dictionary and others for the general public including schools. Monies collected to help this continuing work for the Scottish tongue should be sent to The Secretary, Scottish National Dictionary, 27 George Square, Edinburgh, EH8 9LD.

The National Burns Memorial and Cottage Homes were established in 1896 to mark the centenary of the Poet's death, and comprise 20 houses for the elderly, clustered round a tall turreted tower on the land of Mossgiel farm at Mauchline where Robert Burns worked so hard to hold his family together after his father's death. These cottages surely are just the kind of memorial of which the Poet would have approved - far more to his liking than statues or marble mausoleums. Information about the Memorial Homes and their financial needs is available from The Secretary and Treasurer, The National Burns Memorial and Cottage Homes, c/o Mitchells Roberton, George House, 36 North Hanover Street, Glasgow, G1 2AD.

Although the lassies are always remembered on Burns Night and there are memorials to Highland Mary Campbell, the Poet's wife, Jean Armour, was long neglected until Glasgow and District Burns Association built a group of 10 houses at Mauchline to mark the bicentenary of Burns's birth in 1959. Like the Cottage Homes these Jean Armour Burns Houses were also built on Mossgiel farmland, and they serve a very real need by providing homes for women who are self-sufficient but lack suitable living accommodation. The Association needs funds to maintain these 10 original houses and add to their number. Information can be obtained from the Hon. Secretary, and Treasurer, Jean Armour Burns Houses, c/o Biggart Baillie & Gifford, Dalmore House, 310 St Vincent Street, Glasgow, G2 5QR.

When coffee is finished, announcements made and collections are completed, the Chairman will announce an intermission - 10 to 15 minutes - before the speeches and entertainment begin.

If the programme is to be a long one - and some Burns celebrations can last until two in the morning - then a second interval will follow half way through the entertainment.

THE IMMORTAL MEMORY

The company has reassembled, chairs are set back, glasses are filled, and it is time to get down to the serious business of honouring the memory of Robert Burns. This does not mean two solemn hours - or even two dull hours - of sombre eulogy after which nobody wants to hear the Bard's name mentioned for another twelvemonth.

My own views on this part of Burns Night celebration are mixed. Worship of the Poet to the exclusion of every Scottish writer before or since his time, seems to contradict what the Poet worked for - he was a man who was inspired by writers who preceded him in both Scotland and England. He took an interest even in French thought and Latin literature. Burns was never a nationalist in the narrow meaning of the word - his life stretched far beyond Scotland although he hardly ever crossed the Border. Yet to include the works of others can turn the evening into a kind of St Andrews Night and obscure the real purpose of the January celebration - to honour Robert Burns. Certainly Burns himself admired the work of other poets and songwriters and enjoyed their writings as much as his own, and to that extent he would be the first to want to share the celebration with them.

Perhaps the answer lies somewhere in between. If appropriate, include a song or a poem by another writer, but make sure it is worthy of the evening. Otherwise stick to Burns - After all, if he is honoured in the right way, he will lead on to a greater interest in literature and even in the arts in general. Through Burns a wider audience can be brought to Scotland's great heritage of literature, from the early ballad-makers to present-day poets.

The mood for the Immortal Memory must be right and a couple of Burns songs or a selection of airs to his songs played on the fiddle will set the scene for the Chairman to call on his principal guest to propose the Immortal Memory of Robert Burns.

WHY AN IMMORTAL MEMORY

Before deciding who ought to propose the Immortal Memory it is as well to examine its purpose. It may go without saying that this is a toast to the memory of a great poet, but if it does that and no more, it will be an empty tribute.

What else should this key speech in the Burns Night celebration achieve?

A commentator, writing about the 1859 celebration marking the centenary of the Poet's birth - the first time the Burns movement stretched out to the world in an organised way - gave this reason for Burns's timeless appeal: "It is ... partly because he represents his countrymen more thoroughly in their virtues and their failings than any other man of equal note among them". Few outside Scotland appreciate this, and for that reason they fail to understand properly why the Scots hold the Bard so dear. Burns helps Scots to take stock of themselves, of their way of life and of their fellow men, and the successful proposer of the Immortal Memory will interpret this for his listeners In short, he will act as interpreter between the Poet and today's Scots.

The purpose of the Immortal Memory could be set out as fourfold:

To help people understand what Burns is saying;

To activate them to think about the reasons why Burns said what he did;

To encourage them to apply Burns's values to their own lives and to the social fabric around them. And resolve to improve both;

To persuade them to re-examine their country's nationhood, preserve it, and make it a force for good among their fellow nations.

If the speaker succeeds then he will have inspired his audience to try to rediscover their true selves, to think more kindly about their fellow men, and to want to make the world a better place.

CHOOSING A SPEAKER

Finding a speaker who can command the respect of his listeners and inspire them is not easy. He has to be entertaining enough to hold his audience, yet must not be facile. In the world of Burnsians a large number of people have made a reputation for themselves as good proposers of the Immortal Memory and are invited to travel the world to speak at Anniversary Dinners each year. They are in such demand that they must be booked more than a year in advance, and some even have full diaries for two or more years ahead.

If you can capture such a speaker well and good: if not, there is no need to despair - every community has its quota of good after-dinner speakers, and careful briefing can turn them into successful proposers of the Immortal Memory.

Club secretaries and committee members never pause in the search for a speaker who will enhance their Dinner, and do better than those who make the speeches at rival club celebrations! Although there is plenty of camaraderie among Burns clubs and societies there is always rivalry to run the best Supper in the area. So club members attend other club dinners, listen critically and note names of speakers who ought to be invited to their celebration another year. Burnsians talk among themselves and an efficient secretary will have to be a good listener, a chiel amang his fellow Burnsians taking note of recommended speakers, especially "new faces" for Burns Night.

When a "new face" is found he is quickly asked to pencil into his diary a date a year or two years ahead, when he may be principal guest at the club's Dinner. A hurried consultation with other committee members then enables the secretary to write an official letter of invitation to confirm the provisional booking.

If no speaker comes to mind readily, then the committee ought to meet very soon after one annual dinner to select a principal guest for next year. Debate at this meeting can be hot, and opinions expressed are sometimes worthy of sharper Burns epigrams. There can be dissent over every name on the short list, so that a vote has to be taken and a choice made.

That is how established Burns clubs find speakers: those organising a

Supper for the first time or for a group other that a Burns society will not have the benefit of a committee's broad experience, and will have to rely on their own ability to find the right person. Here the famous Burns "grapevine" will help.

By talking to other people names of possible principal guests will emerge, and with luck some of these names will recur. These are the ones to consider seriously, although one must avoid the trap of choosing somebody who is an entertaining speaker, but cares nothing for Burns.

If no suitable person can be found locally, then look further afield, discuss the problem with other Burns societies or with the Federation in Kilmarnock. The Burns movement is a brotherhood, and will always help fellow organisations.

If the worst comes to the worst then you will have to fall back on a local personality with no reputation as a Burns speaker; choose a Scot if possible, say a civic leader, a newspaper editor, or a leading businessman - somebody with "go" about him, but don't assume that a man who can run the most prosperous factory in the district can make a good speech. Especially a speech about Robert Burns! Choose a person you have heard speak yourself if possible, and if you are in the way of attending dinners (Burns or others) listen critically whenever you go to a function, read local press reports, and listen to people being interviewed on the radio or television. In that way you can build up you own "bank" of speakers.

Having selected your possible speaker, arrange to meet him, talk to him about Burns, find out how much he is in sympathy with the Poet and his ideals. Explain to him the background of your own organisation, its objectives, and the reasons why it is holding a Burns Supper. In discussion you will be able to assess how willingly he will accept being briefed and how well he is likely to perform on "The Night".

If you are satisfied that he measures up to your needs. ask him to put the date in his diary provisionally, then follow up with a confirmatory letter, giving full details - date, place and time of dinner, maximum length of time he will be expected to speak, names of other speakers if you know them, and suggest a date for a briefing meeting a month or six weeks in advance of the event.

What happens if your speaker is taken ill or is delayed by the notoriously bad weather which always seems to plague Burns Suppers? The answer is to be prepared to make the speech yourself or to warn a committee member that he may be called on - Of course if you have a few days notice you can usually find another Burnsian to propose the toast. But never assume that you will not need a substitute until you actually see your principal guest walk into the room. Only then can you tell his understudy to relax.

BRIEFING THE SPEAKER

Briefing should not be left to the Chairman alone: a small group of committee members should meet him informally to explain to him his part in the proceedings. You will have already told him something about your own organisation, but a reminder is no bad thing now, so take along whatever printed literature you have to leave with him. Remind him of the type of anniversary dinner it is to be - formal or informal; a serious meeting of knowledgeable Burnsians, or just folk with a passing interest in the Poet; a male gathering or mixed company; whether dress is formal or informal. Jog his memory about how long you expect him to talk, who the other speakers are, what entertainment will follow, what other guests are expected, and lastly remind him of the time of the dinner and the people he can expect to meet. Put yourself in his place and ask what you would like to know if you were in his place and you will not go far wrong.

On "the Night" your speaker will no doubt be nervous, so spare him as many surprises as you can. At one of the first anniversary dinners I ever addressed I discovered after I had sat down at the table that one of the guests was an important Burns Federation office-bearer. No one had thought to mention that he was to be present, or to introduce me to him during the pre-dinner reception, and as a result I spent a miserable two hours until my speech was over, worrying about what this man who knew so much about Burns was going to think of my empty words. Only later, I discovered that he was a delightful man with a mind open enough to listen to a beginner like me!

HOW LONG SHOULD IT BE?

Most serious Burns Clubs ask for an Immortal Memory of 30 - 35 minutes and I have known a speaker to hold his audience spellbound for almost and hour. However, a far more acceptable length for the average speaker and average audience is 20 - 25 minutes.

YOU HAVE BEEN ASKED TO SPEAK

This book is designed to help the person who has been asked to speak at a Burns Supper as much as for the person who is organising the event. Now it is time to throw the speaker a lifeline.

Before you begin to compile your speech let me offer a few general hints. Clear diction, a well modulated voice and a pace which allows listeners to assimilate what is being said are all essential ingredients of any speech, whether about Robert Burns or life in Babylonian times. Again it must be emphasised that length is vital: the speech must not be so long that it needs to be gabbled through to reach the end within reasonable time. So practise it thoroughly at home to get these basic points right.

Those who are fortunate enough to live within reach of the Burns Country would find inspiration by walking around the places connected with the Bard. Go to Alloway early in the day before other tourists arrive and stand beside the ingle to picture the family's daily life; stand by the Poet's father's grave in the Auld Kirk of Alloway and think about the relationship between father and son; feel the wind in your face on the high arch of the Brig O'Doon; and visit the Tam O' Shanter Experience to see the audio-visual interpretation of his life. There are other places to visit - Mount Oliphant, Leglen Wood, Lochlea, Mossgiel, Mauchline Kirk, or the banks of the rivers Ayr, Doon or Nith, and of course Ellisland and the Poet's house at Dumfries. An hour's crack with the curator of one of the houses in which Burns lived would be time will spent. Visit one or all of these places and use a little imagination to visualise Burns's time and lifestyle. If you read about the Poet his life and achievement will suddenly come into focus. And read the poems, then read them again.

When it comes to writing the speech, bear in mind Burns's own humility, and as a reminder set in front of you the words:

> *O wad some Power the giftie gie us*
> *tae see oursels as ithers see us!*

With that in mind you will not go far astray.

SUITABLE SUBJECTS

Like a sermon, a good Immortal Memory should start from a text, but there the kirk comparison should end. The speech should examine the theme and relate it to the audience, quoting generously from Burns to underline the points being made. It should contain light and shadow, but end with the Poet bathed in a blaze.

Burns clubs expect their speaker to focus on an aspect of the Poet's life, and use it to demonstrate the great achievement of Robert Burns and the debt the world owes to him. Here is a selection of themes from Burns Suppers round the world taken at random from a single edition of the Burns Chronicle.

Burns - Ploughman or genius and intellectual;
Burns as a Man;
Exciseman and Farmer;
Folksong writer of genius;
Burns's thoughts if he were alive today;
Burns - Preserver of our heritage;
Farming in Ayrshire in Burns's time;
Dominies in Burns's day (speech by a schoolmaster);
Hame (at an exiles' Dinner)

Whatever the subject, the aim should be to relate it to the audience and to the Poet's work. The first step towards this is to read as widely as possible round the subject, taking in the views of Burns and others. Pay especial heed to what the Bard had to say and what comments others made on his views during his lifetime or after. Read the classic biographies of the Poet by Hans Hecht, Catherine Carswell, and Franklyn Bliss Snyder as well as more recent ones by James Mackay and Ian McIntyre. Follow that up with specialist books and articles on the subject you have chosen. Read the poems, both to set the mood for writing about Burns, and to find suitable quotations to illustrate your speech.

Here are ideas for a few Immortal Memories to show how subjects might be tackled. The same principles can be applied to any other topic or theme to produce an Immortal Memory, which will come over to the audience as fresh and interesting. Remember these are not finished speeches, only outlines around which your own Immortal Memory can be built.

OUTLINE SPEECHES

1 THE FARMER POET

Relating the life story of the Bard is considered the easiest Immortal Memory for beginners, yet it can be the hardest one to hold the interest of listeners because it covers well-trodden ground.

Rather than recite all the facts in chronological order you can give this speech a lift by choosing a single theme from Burns's life and confining your talk to that. For example, you could take the words of Maria Riddell which at once admitted the imperfections of the Poet's life yet pointed to his genius - your text might be: "It is only on the gem we are disturbed to see the dust. The pebble may be soiled, and we do not regard it".

Consider this statement against four periods of his life:
farm lad;
famous man
man in love with mankind and womankind;
and sick man struggling to fulfil his destiny.

Farm lad: Brother Gilbert suggests a rather lonely, inward looking boyhood when he says, "We rarely saw anybody but the members of our own family. There were no boys of our age, or near it, in the neighbourhood . . . My father was for some time almost the only companion we had." He also suggests that his brother tended to be jealous of others who were more fortunate than himself.

Yet Robert himself talks of meetings with young people in Ayr; of lessons with his teacher, John Murdoch; and, as he grew to early manhood, of the Bachelors' Club debating society which he helped to found in Tarbolton, the dancing classes he attended - to his father's annoyance - and the full social life he managed to maintain while working long hard hours on the farm.

The Cotter's Saturday Night does not suggest an introverted young man or an introverted family:

> *With joy unfeign'd, brothers and sisters meet,*
>   *And each for other's weelfare kindly spiers:*   *asks
> *The social hours, swift-wing'd, unnottic'd fleet*
>   *Each tells the uncos* that he sees or hears.*   *news
> *The Parents partial eye their hopeful years;*
>   *Anticipation forward points the view;*
> *The mother wi' her needle and her sheers*
>   *Gars auld claes look amaist as weel's the new;*
> *The father mixes a' wi' admonition due.*

Contrast this with satire against the Church and against injustice. Burns was in trouble with the Kirk because of his youthful love affairs; without these he would still have quarrelled with the Kirk or with a section of it at least, because he could not bear the narrowness of strict Calvinism or hypocrisy. He satirised religion's least attractive features in *The Holy Fair,* one of a series of poems which caused a great furore throughout the countryside. Burns painted pictures so clearly in his poems that folk could see themselves reflected in his words.

> *Here some are thinkin on their sins,*
>   *An some upon their claes;*
> *Ane curses feet that fyl'd* his shins,*   *dirtied
>   *Anither sighs an prays:*
> *On this hand sits a chosen swatch,*
>   *Wi screw'd-up grace-proud faces;*
> *On that a set o chaps, at watch,*
>   *Thrang* winkin at the lasses*   *busy
> *To chairs that day.*

Small wonder the Kirk was alarmed. Then he set upon one of its most hypocritical elders, William Fisher, who had led an attack on Burns's friend and landlord Gavin Hamilton. *Holy Willie's Prayer* shows the young Burns at his sharp-tongued best as he satirised the elder who knew he was among those chosen for salvation. Its impossible to read the poem without hearing Holy Willie's voice, high-pitched and sanctimonious.

Yet I am here, a chosen sample,
  To shew Thy grace is great and ample:
I'm here, a pillar of thy Temple
  Strong as a rock,
A guide, a buckler and example
  To a' thy flock.

It's to Burns's credit that *Holy Willie's Prayer* was written to defend his friend Gavin Hamilton, rather than his own personal attack on Willie Fisher. *The Twa Dugs* was an angry reaction to the lawsuit his father faced over the farm lease at Lochlea, again pointing to the poet's humanity in understanding the suffering of the poor farmer.

I've notic'd, on our Laird's court-day,
  (An mony a time my heart's been wae),
Poor tenant-bodies, scant o' cash,
  How they maun thole* a factor's snash;   *suffer
He'll stamp an threaten, curse an swear,
  He'll apprehend them, poind their gear,
While they maun stand, wi' aspect humble,
  An' hear it a', an fear an' tremble.

Already we see the gem gleaming through.

Famous man: Fame came suddenly to Robert Burns. One day he is a farm lad fleeing the wrath of the kirk and of James Armour whose daughter he had made pregnant. Next he is author of a best-seller, a book of poems that everybody is clamouring to read, and is on his way to Edinburgh to negotiate another volume. The pebble has indeed proved to be a gemstone, clearly reflecting its colours through the dust of disgrace because of overfondness for the lassies and the sharp tongue with which he criticised the less attractive aspects of the life around him.

In Edinburgh Robert Burns presented the outward appearance of a mere ploughman with little education, but few were taken in: they recognised his true genius. He himself was apprehensive about mixing with the great men of the capital, although he felt in no way inferior to them. Burns always knew where he stood. He wrote: "Never did Saul's armour sit so heavy on David when going to encounter Goliath, as does the encumbering robe of public notice with which the friendship and patronage of some 'names to fame' have invested me - I do not say this in the ridiculous idea of seeming self-abasement, and affected modesty.- I have long studied myself, and I think I know pretty exactly what ground I occupy, both as a Man and a Poet.

He went through the motions of praising the city in his *Address to Edinburgh*, yet must often have thought at this time of the words of another "address" of his, *The Address to the Unco Guid* which applied to that smug society.

> O ye wha are sae guid yoursel,
>   Sae pious and sae holy,
> Ye've nought to do but mark and tell
>   Your neebours' fauts and folly!

Sometimes his pen wounded others deeply, but those were the very moments when he could turn about and say something which showed true humanity, humility and understanding. In that same poem *The Unco Guid:*

> Then gently scan your brother man,
>   Still gentler sister woman;
> Tho they may gang a kennin* wrang   *little
>   To step aside is human:
> One point must still be greatly dark.
>   The moving Why they do it;
> And just as lamely can ye mark,
>   How far perhaps they rue it.
>
> Who made the heart, 'tis He alone
>   Decidedly can try us,
> He knows each chord, its various tone,
>   Each spring its various bias:
> Then at the balance let's be mute,
>   We never can adjust it;
> What's done we partly may compute,
> But know not what's resisted.

The dust of sharp criticism is at once swept away by perfect understanding.

The man in love: Burns has plenty of critics who can be quoted here, from his own family's despair over the all-too-apparent results of his love-making to the strictures of his first biographer, Dr. James Currie. And the Poet himself can be cited in support of or against his weakness for womankind. "My heart was compleatly (sic) tinder and was eternally lighted up by some Goddess or other", he wrote once. Yet there is ample evidence that women sought out Burns as much as he ever sought them.

Burns's love ran to more than broken hearts and illegitimate children. From it flowed songs and poems describing every aspect of the emotion from a young girl's plea that she's "owre young to marry yet" to the companionship of old age in *John Anderson My Jo*.

> John Anderson my jo, John,
>> We clamb the hill thegither;
> And mony a cantie* day, John,   *happy
>> We've had wi ane anither:
> Now we maun totter down, John,
>> And hand in hand we'll go;
> And sleep thegither at the foot,
>> Jonn Anderson, my Jo.

The sick man: Here Burns needed all the compassion he had poured out to others, and he was ill rewarded by his first biographer. Dr. Currie wrote that Burns's drinking affected his work, but this is nonsense. Burns was highly thought of by his Excise colleagues and when someone tried to denounce him to the powers in Edinburgh, nothing was found against him. Burns's drinking was social - it was company he craved not whisky. Indeed his health could not have stood up to excessive drinking.

The glorious drunkenness of *Willie Brew'd a Peck o' Maut* is not the singing of the drunkard but the carousal of the man who enjoys company and a dram, but just occasionally drifts aver the edge of sobriety.

> We are na' fou,* we're nae that fou,   *drunk
> But just a drappie in our e'e!
> The cock may craw, the day may daw,
> And ay we'll taste the barley bree!*   whisky

From each aspect of his life Burns created poetry which is a distillation of compassion, understanding and love for his fellow man. Even where his own life can be exposed to criticism he disarms his critics. The dust truly shows up the gem that lies underneath it.

In Burns's frailty can be found the basis of his immortality: where there appear to be depths, heights suddenly appear, where weakness shows through, strength can be found.

Maria Riddell saw the true Burns, the man who inspires us still today, the man to whom we humbly offer our Immortal Memory.

OUTLINE SPEECH 2
PLOUGHMAN OR INTELLECTUAL

This Immortal Memory can take as its theme the note Alison Chalmers sent to a friend after seeing Burns in Edinburgh. "The town is at present agog with the ploughman poet who receives adulation with native dignity, and is the very figure of his profession - strong and coarse - but has a most enthusiastic heart of LOVE".

The speech will contrast the farming background with Edinburgh society and show how Burns was remarkably well educated - schooled beyond most of his equals. By his genius he was able to turn book learning into original thoughts and opinions which reached the core of man's being.

From early days he was a thinker, using his mind and forming his own point of view. He told how one of the first things he remembered was seeing a pretty young maidservant in church being forced to rise to make way for the fat, pompous son of the local mansion house. And Burns carried that picture in his mind ever after. No doubt that was the seed of *A Man's a Man for A' That*.

> Ye see yon birkie* ca'd a lord,
> Wha struts, and stares, and a' that
> Though hundreds worship at his word,
> He's but a cuif* for a' that   *fool
> For a' that, and a' that,
> His ribband, star, and a' that,
> The man o independent mind,
> He looks and laughs at a' that.

He showed early signs of intellectual agility in arguments with his friends, in his poems lambasting hypocrisy within the Church, and of course in helping to establish the Bachelors' Club debating society in Tarbolton.

In Edinburgh he was Daniel in the lion's den. Yet he was not overawed by the great minds of that period which history remembers as Edinburgh's Golden Age. He was confident of his own ability because he had thought out where he stood and he knew that he deserved respect. Burns was aware that he was miles further ahead of those he met intellectually than his crude Ayrshire farming manners suggested, yet he was behind them socially. And, though people generally accepted his own presentation of himself as an unlettered ploughman, there were plenty of great men in the capital who recognised his true intellectual capacity.

Yet Burns was never at home among such society, and was drawn to the Crochallan Fencibles drinking club rather than to the drawing rooms of the New Town. He was also pulled towards writing in the Doric instead of Augustan stanzas in standard English. Even his great and passionate love affair in Edinburgh with Agnes Maclehose, was conducted on a high formal plane with Burns calling himself Sylvander and her Clarinda. Yet the affair produced a basic love song of deep human feeling, *Ae Fond Kiss*.

> I'll ne'er blame my partial fancy:
> Naething could resist my Nancy!
> But to see her was to love her,
> Love but her, and love for ever.

> *Had we never lov'd sae kindly,*
> *Had we never lov'd sae blindly,*
> *Never met - or never parted -*
> *We had ne'er been broken-hearted.*

Proof of the brilliance of Burns's intellect is found in the fact that people with brilliant minds sought him out for his company and for his conversation - rich, influential, important people. Because Burns was the type of man that he was, Robert Graham of Fintry helped him to become an Exciseman and for the same reason Patrick Miller offered him the lease of Ellisland farm.

Burns's genius shines through his poetry, perhaps as brilliantly in *Tam O'Shanter* as in any other poem. Here he took a simple folk-tale and fashioned it into a great narrative poem, brilliantly constructed, written with genius. Examine the poem, in its various parts - the simplicity with which the scene is set in Ayr, the clarity with which Tam is described, the vividness of the hellish ongoings at Alloway's Auld Haunted Kirk.

> *Warlocks and witches in a dance;*
> *Nae cotillion, brent* new frae France*   *brand
> *But hornpipes, jigs, strathspeys, and reels,*
> *Put life and mettle in their heels.*
> *A winnock-bunker* in the east,*   *window seat
> *There sat Auld Nick, in shape o beast;*
> *A touzie tyke,* black, grim and large,*   *unkempt dog
> *To gie them music was his charge:*
> *He screw'd the pipes and gart* them skirl,*   *made
> *Till roof and rafters a' did dirl.**   *rattle

The search for the intellectual Robert Burns can be taken much further - to fit him in his niche among Scottish men of letters, to examine the elements of his work which are derived from earlier poets and literary sources.

His contemporaries were shrewd enough to recognise his genius, and to accept the "uneducated ploughman" as their intellectual superior, even if a few held back socially.

Burns allowed the ploughman myth to persist when he could easily have scotched it. Why? Because it suited him to be thought a rustic genius by those who were not bright enough to recognise what he really was. Burns was a shrewd man who knew when to be the intellectual and when to be the ploughman with a talent for scribbling verse. And, oddly he was at home in both roles.

Why should he not have been? For far too long the farm worker has been regarded as beneath his townsmen peers, and it is only now that his true worth is being acknowledged. In Burns's time his work was endless and grinding and his reward miserly. Burns lifted him to a higher plane.

The truth is that Burns was both ploughman and intellectual, and it is as both that we salute him.

OUTLINE SPEECH 3
THOUGHTS ON THE MILLENNIUM

Burns would have had plenty to say on the millennium - no doubt in verse. At the centenary of his birth one of his sons said that the Poet once remarked to his wife, 'Jean, one hundred years hence they'll think mair o' me than they do now.' He was right. Two hundred years on they thought more of him - and at the start of the new century we can say with confidence that if the world survives, a thousand years from now folk will think even more of him.

Why? Because Robert Burns is timeless, just as the way the world behaves is timeless. He was as involved in politics and boastfully patriotic as the next man, but he combined this with humility and humanity.

Our veneer of civilisation is woesomely thin - so thin that we see through the cracks the suffering we inflict on one another. The twentieth century brought the most wonderful inventions and medical discoveries to promote a better life, yet it also saw the greatest wars ever known.

Burns would have had comment to make on that. He would also have had plenty to say about man's inhumanity to man in everyday life, about common decency, and about brotherly love. And he would offer pity and understanding - and without grand language or symbols. The daisy and the mouse at Mossgiel were all he needed to point to the fate of himself and of mankind.

Thy wee-bit housie, too, in ruin!
Its silly wa's the win's are strewin'!
An naething, now, to a big new ane,
O' foggage green!
An bleak December's winds ensuin',
Baith snell* an' keen!   **cold*

The cruelty of mankind is underlined by the animal's hopelessness, but Burns quickly points out that for human beings the fear and misery have an added dimension because man is God's created, greater being:

Still, thou art blest, compar'd wi' me!
The present only toucheth thee:
But och! I backward cast my e'e
On prospects drear!
An forward, tho I canna see,
I guess an fear!

Through the years right down to today, Burns speaks clearly to us and points out our own hopes and fears. If only mankind would listen to him and learn. Perhaps in drinking to Robert Burns's Immortal Memory tonight we can make a start.

He had many disappointments and failings - and was the first to recognise them: he could be driven to despair or lose his temper easily. Anyone who has suffered the delays of officialdom and slow builders will recognise a chord of sympathy in Burns's worry when he was trying to hasten the building of his farmhouse at Ellisland so that he could be reunited with his wife Jean, and their family:

"I am distressed with the want of my house in the most provoking manner! he wrote to the builder. "It loses me two hours' work every day, besides other inconveniences. For God's sake let me but within the shell of it". And the relief when he was finally settled in it with his wife Jean and able to sing:

O were I on Parnassus hill,
Or had o Helicon my fill;
That I might catch poetic skill,
To sing how dear I love thee!

Like the rest of us he could take umbrage easily and forgive equally easily. When the landlord at the inn in Inverary was too busy with the Duke of Argyll's guests to serve him, he wrote:

There's naething here but Highland pride,
And Highland scab and hunger,
If Providence has sent me here,
'Twas surely in an anger.

Yet the same man could also write a touching little note of thanks:

When death's dark stream I ferry o'er,
A time that surely shall come;
In Heaven itself, I'll ask no more,
Than just a Highland welcome.

These apparently irreconcilable views are exactly like our own veering, inconsistent attitudes. Today Burns speaks as clearly as if he were with us still.

But most important of all is his ability to reassure us of our own worth - to tell us that 'the man's the gowd for a' that.' There are no better words than those of Robert Burns to take us through the whole of the next millennium:

Then let us pray that come it may
(As come it will for a' that),
That Sense and Worth o'er a' the earth,
Shall bear the gree* an a' that.   *have priority

For a' that, an a' that,
It's comin yet for a' that,
That man to man, the world, o'er
Shall brithers be for a' that.

That is Robert Burns's message for the twenty-first century.

OUTLINE SPEECH 4
LOOKING HOMEWARDS

A favourite (and appropriate) subject for exiles, and one I have used in Scotland to remind Scots of what living outside Scotland means to those of us who are in "foreign parts", even if only across the Border in England.

Many suitable quotes can be found in Burns's works from which to examine what home means to the Scot - for example one of the Jacobite songs such as *The Highland Widow's Lament* which begins "Oh, I am come to the low Countrie," or *It was a' for our Rightfu' King*. But why not start from someone else's view? Where better than the *Canadian Boat Song*, that anonymous poem which expresses longing for home more movingly than most poems about exile?

> *From the lone shieling of the misty island*
> *Mountains divide us, and the waste of seas -*
> *Yet still the blood is strong, the heart is Highland,*
> *And we in dreams behold the Hebrides.*

This is a reminder both of what exile means and of the uneasy times in which Burns lived and it is easy to bridge two centuries to our own shifting times. Social change forced thousands to leave - unwilling emigrants - although one must not lose sight of the many adventurous Scots who through the centuries have willingly ventured overseas in search of fortune.

Burns himself came close to emigrating on two occasions: to Jamaica to escape the wrath of Jean Armour's father, and to London where he was offered work as a journalist. That he stayed in Scotland was perhaps the most fortunate thing that happened for our country in all its history - apart from Bannockburn! Burns loved his homeland and he loved his home. He recognised the importance of family life and values and he summed these up in *"The Cotter's Saturday Night"*, the poem which means family life to the Scot:

Belyve, the elder bairns come drapping in,
At service out, among the farmers roun';
Some ca' the pleugh, some herd, some tentie* rin   *carefully
A cannie errand to a neebor town:
Their eldest hope, their Jenny, woman grown,
In youthfu' bloom, love sparkling in her e'e,
Comes hame, perhaps to show a braw new gown,
Or deposits her sair-won penny-fee,
To help her parents dear, if they in hardship be.

Burns concerned himself with all aspects of life in Scotland - political, religious and social. He spelt out clearly where he thought each failed the people, a brave thing to do in the 18th century when autocratic governments had powers to silence their critics. Are there not parallels to be found today?

Burns's greatest gift to the exile, however, was to preserve his heritage and give it a timelessness which extends across the globe and even across generations. Two main ingredients of this are his songs and language.

Songs: Burns revived the all-but-lost tradition of folk song. He wrote over 300 songs, many of them new versions of older ones, many of them new words to traditional airs going back even beyond the Reformation. Here he was exposing something which lay below the surface of consciousness, and naturally Scottish hearts responded.

Language: Like all creative young men, Burns experimented before settling on a way of expressing himself which suited him best. He tried standard English but rejected it for the vernacular, and we should be thankful he did. Language is a key ingredient in the preservation of any nation's identity.

Decent values, the Scots tongue and Burns's heritage of song were almost all that many Scots had to take with them when they sailed to make new lives in other parts of the world. But these were enough to make home a magnet to which thoughts were drawn even after several generations, when completely integrated into their new homelands.

THE OTHER SPEECHES

Only two other speeches are obligatory - the Toast to the Lassies and the Response to that toast. An Appreciation of the Immortal Memory is usually given also, and is a courtesy which the principal speaker appreciates. I have been to dinners where, instead of an appreciation of the Immortal Memory, the speaker has been invited later on in the evening to say a few words in appreciation of the club, but on the whole I believe it is better for a show of appreciation of the Immortal Memory to be given.

The length of these speeches will depend on the rest of the programme, the formality of the whole celebration, and perhaps on which other organisations are present and have to be recognised. Regardless of all these factors, however, the Lassies toast and reply should never extend beyond about ten minutes. Six to seven minutes is ideal, with the reply slightly shorter.

But how do you stop a speaker when he is in full flow? You don't; you suffer. It is easier to stop him before he begins, if that doesn't sound too Irish. When you invite him, make it clear that he will have six minutes and must not talk beyond that allotted time. Refer to this limit in his letter of invitation, remind him again when he is briefed a month or so before the dinner, and give him a detailed programme for the evening, including timings. On the night itself slip in another firm, friendly reminder. If anyone overruns his time after that, never never invite him again, and don't recommend him to anyone else.

When you are asking other Clubs about possible speakers always find out whether they are men who habitually overrun their time, and in return when you are asked to advise on speakers, make it clear whether they can be trusted to follow the programme timing. There is nothing worse for guests and organiser alike than to find the programme over-running by half an hour or more, so that some of the entertainment has to be dropped, which is not fair to the audience or artistes - a long-winded bore is no substitute for a couple of Burns songs.

The Immortal Memory is the serious work of the evening: The other speeches, apart from the Appreciation, are the fun. They should therefore be lighthearted and humorous, and aim to entertain every bit as much as the songs and recitations among which they are interspersed.

THE APPRECIATION

This is usually given by a member of the company with a deep knowledge of Burns, who will speak briefly (say five minutes) on the topic which the proposer has chosen, reminding the company of salient points and of the relevance of the Bard to their lives, as referred to in the speech. He will thank the proposer and naturally, if the job has been done well, give fulsome praise. The Appreciation is brief, but it is important because it lends extra authority to what has been said in the Immortal Memory.

THE LASSIES

If there is a joker in the pack, play him now! The Toast to the Lassies should be the most amusing speech of the evening.

I notice that some programmes say "Lassies" and other "Lasses". Which is correct? Both in fact, and the only explanation of the difference which I can offer is that "Lasses" is the plural of the word "lass" which is a standard English word. "Lassie", on the other hand, is purely Scottish. For that reason I prefer the programme to say, "The Lassies".

If you cannot make up your mind which you prefer you can entitle the toast "Bonnie Jean" and associate it with the Poet's wife and wifely virtue in general.

The toast varies according to whether the dinner is all-male or mixed company. If there are women present then it is a speech teasing womenfolk for their shortcoming as pointed out by Burns. There are plenty of examples from which to choose - from Tam O' Shanter's wife to the strong-minded landlady with whom the Poet lodged on his first visit to Edinburgh; from Maria Riddell's teasing of his emotions to Willie Wastle's harridan at Linkumdoddie.

Willie Wastle dwalt on Tweed,
The spot they ca'd it Linkumdoddie,
Willie was a wabster guid
Could stown a clue wi onie body;
He had a wife was dour and din,
O, Tinkler Maidgie was her mither,
Sic a wife as Willie had,
I wad na gie a button for her.

This should be a racy speech, with plenty of jokes and fun poked at womankind in our society. There's a lot of scope in these feminist days and laws which forbid one from advertising for a charwoman or even a chairwoman.

Gentle fun is the key to this speech, and it must always end on a complimentary note, again referring to Burns, his patient, understanding wife, and his basic respect for the female sex. A superb song to link Burns's feelings on womankind is *Of A' The Airts The Wind Can Blow:*

Of a' the airts the wind can blaw
I dearly like the west,
For there the bonie lassie lives,
The lassie I lo'e best.
There wild woods grow, and rivers row
And monie a hill between,
But day and night my fancy's flight
Is ever with my Jean.

I see her in the dewy flowers-
I see her sweet and fair.
I hear her in the tunefu birds-
I hear her charm the air.
There's not a bonie flower that springs
By fountain, shaw, or green,
There's not a bonie bird that sings,
But minds me o my Jean.

At the end of his speech the proposer will ask the men to rise and join him in drinking the toast to the Lassies.

THE RESPONSE

The toast to the Lassies is a battle of the sexes, and in the response, women have a chance to have their revenge. Now they can take men to task for their shortcomings, especially their chauvinism, drinking and abuse of woman's love for them. Burns can be used to back this up too, especially to make the point that without the lassies, man seldom amounts to very much in life .

No matter what may have been said about the lassies, Burns give them the unanswerable retort to the menfolk. In *Green Grow the Rashes o* he writes:

> *Auld Nature swears, the lovely Dears*
> *Her noblest work she classes, O*
> *Her prentice han' she try'd on man,*
> *An' then she made the lasses, O.*

Behind most successful men there is a woman which of course was true of Burns, who had Jean Armour. Take away the lassies and what would be left of Burns's songs? Thus the speech will end by complimenting the opposite sex.

In cold print the toast to the Lassies may sound an outdated, chauvinist display, out of tune with modern life. In practice it is a highly enjoyable part of the evening, which still goes down well,

OTHER TOASTS

The number of other speeches will depend on the nature of the occasion and who is present. If a civic leader is attending, then obviously it would be respectful to toast his town or area and it would flatter him to be given the chance to speak. On the programme this goes under many titles, "Our Town", "The City of .....", "Oor Toon", and so on. At Dinners where the majority of those attending are exiled Scots, the toast becomes "The Town of our Adoption", or even "The Land of our Adoption".

This toast can be combined with a general toast to all the guests if the number of speeches is limited.

Scotland features as a toast on many Burns Night programmes, and rightly so. Titles vary according to taste - "Scotland", "Scotia", "Auld Scotland", "Auld Scotia", or even "Puir Auld Scotland". Overseas, this toast becomes "The Land we Left". At exiles' Dinners it is right to honour the country in which the celebration is taking place, so a toast to "Land of our Adoption" is appropriate, or one coupling that country with Scotland, under the title "Two Lands".

The Burns movement is included in the toast list of many organisations - "The Robert Burns World Federation" or "Kindred Clubs". And if a prominent Federation representative is present this will give him the chance to respond and talk about the aims and achievements of the Federation and of the Burns movement generally.

SANGS AND CLATTER

Remember how in Tam O'Shanter the "night drave on wi' sangs and clatter; And ay the ale was growing better"? That's how a Burns Night should go, with plenty of songs and music and recitations to follow the meal and formal speeches. No particular works of Burns have to be included, but clubs have their own favourites which frequently appear on their programme.

Tam O' Shanter is probably the most popular poem for Burns Night recitation, with *Holy Willie's Prayer* and the *Address to the Unco Guid* as alternatives. *The Cotter's Saturday Night* is another which goes down well, but of course it is always good to surprise the company with something "different", like *Death and Dr Hornbrook* or perhaps *The Twa Dogs* recited as a duologue.

If you have a really good performer available try a longer poem by all means, but if you are uncertain about the quality of your verse speaker than select two shorter poems rather than one long one, and space them well apart in the programme.

As there are usually a number of non-Burnsians present at any dinner, it is a good idea when introducing the poem to say a few words about its origins and to explain what it is about.

Songs and Burns can never be separated. He wrote more than three hundred of them, practically every one a gem, and ranging from love and drinking songs to patriotic and political. And many of them are set to traditional old Scottish airs. No wonder the Burns Night celebrations often end with someone regretting that a particular favourite has been missed out.

The only advice to be given on choosing appropriate songs for a Burns

Night programme is that they should cover a wide range of Burns's themes to display his genius. Otherwise, be guided by whatever your singers feel they can sing best, or if you are anxious to include a certain song, then find a performer who can put it over well.

One way of reminding the audience of the range of Burns's song-writing achievement is to include a selection of airs to the songs as a solo instrumental item, perhaps while the guests assemble, during service of coffee, or as an item between speeches.

I have already referred to the works of others (page 56) and I see no harm in these provided they do not obscure Burns's own writings. The only plea I would make is that they should be the work of writers of worth Unfortunately many anniversary dinners take place at which the principal guest gives a splendid oration, only to find that, apart from a few Burns songs, no other reference is made to the Bard or his works. This is fine as a club evening, but it isn't a Burns Supper.

And poems or songs written by others about Burns sometimes appear on Burns Night Programmes - often the work of earnest folk who genuinely want to honour the Bard, but which fall so far short in quality that they would be better omitted. The fact that they are presented on Burns Night alongside those of Burns merely serves to underline their shallowness and poor craftsmanship. That kind of "work by others" can well be dispensed with on Burns Night!

Let all the guests participate in the fun of the evening by joining in the choruses of the songs, or even by singing a few of the songs together. But if that is to be done, make it an official part of the proceedings, and have the words duplicated or printed so that nobody has to hum or worse still get the words wrong.

There is one song about Burns which many clubs consider a "must" for their programme - *The Star o' Robbie Burns*. The *Star* was written by James Thomson, first president of Hawick Burns Club, who was born at Bowden on the Borders in 1827 and who developed such a love of the Poet that he carried a tattered Kilmarnock edition of Burns's poems in his pocket while he herded cows as a boy. Thomson published a volume of poems, but it is by *The Star* that he is remembered. Music for the song is by James Booth.

THE STAR O' ROBBIE BURNS

Words by James Thomson Music by James Booth

There is a star whose beaming ray
Is shed on ev'ry clime
It shines by night, it shines by day
And ne'er grows dim wi' time
It rose upon the banks of Ayr,
It shone on Doon's clear stream -
A hundred years are gane and mair,
Yet brighter grows its beam.

Chorus

Let kings and courtiers rise and fa',
This world has mony turns
But brightly beams aboon them a'
The star o' Robbie Burns.

Though he was but a ploughman lad
And wore the hodden grey,
Auld Scotland's sweetest bard was bred
Aneath a roof o' strae
To sweep the strings o' Scotia's lyre
It needs nae classic lore;
It's mither wit an native fire
That warms the bosom's core.

Chorus

On fame's emblazon'd page enshrin'd
His name is foremost now,
And many a costly wreath's been twin'd
To grace his honest brow
And Scotland's heart expands wi' joy
Whene'er the day returns
That gave the world its peasant boy -
Immortal Robbie Burns.

The time to bring the anniversary celebrations to an end is while the company is asking for more songs, recitations and music. In that way a few may be tempted to open their copy of Burns's Poems (and every Scottish household contains one) when they return home and read some for themselves.

If a dance is to follow to round off the evening there may be some who will not want to stay on, so the Chairman should now wind up the formal part of the celebration.

First he will call on an official of the Club to thank the speakers and performers formally and express the thanks of the Club to the Chairman and secretary or organiser of the Dinner, and others connected with the success of the evening.

A guest may respond very briefly - a few words only - to express the appreciation of his fellow guests for the happy evening.

The Chairman now calls on the company to sing *Auld Lang Syne*.

This song, more than any other, means Robert Burns to the world, It has been translated into dozens of languages and is sung round the globe by people who have never heard of Burns. *Auld Lang Syne* is recognised universally as a song of warmly remembered friendship and as a song of parting, but in Scotland, especially on Burns Night it takes on far deeper meaning. To us it is a reminder of our roots, of the land and traditions which made us what we are. When the Bard refers in this song to running about the braes and paddling in the burn everyone conjures up his own vision of the scene. For me, the burn is the one which flows gently into the river Doon just below Minishant in Ayrshire, and the braes are the Whinnie Knowe which overlooks the village. I never read or sing these verses of *Auld Lang Syne* without feeling the warmth of childhood summers there more than a generation ago. However the song evokes more than nostalgia: in it Burns uses remembrance of times and places past to look forward to a future full of hope.

> *And there's a hand, my trusty fiers!**   *companion
> *And gie's a hand o'thine*
> *And we'll tak a right gude-willie waught,**   drink
> *For Auld lang syne.*

The mechanics of singing *Auld Lang Syne* arouse as much passion in Scottish hearts as calling the British Isles *England* or putting sugar on your porridge. Scots complain bitterly about non Scots singing "zyne" when they mean "syne", yet one hears these selfsame complainers sing "for the sake of auld land syne" where Burns wrote simply "for auld lang syne", and they sing "we'll meet again some ither night" which are not the words which Burns wrote.

Is it asking too much of anyone who is devoting a whole evening to honouring the Poet at a Burns Supper to spend half an hour beforehand running through the words - even committing them to memory? Everybody *nearly* knows *Auld Lang Syne* - but as we used to say as children "Nearly never kill'd a man". Perhaps not, but it has certainly murdered *Auld Lang Syne* many times over.

Here is Burns's version of the song:

> *Should Auld acquaintance be forgot*
>   *And never brought to mind?*
> *Should Auld acquaintance be forgot*
>   *And auld lang syne.*

Chorus:

> *For auld lang syne, my jo,*
>   *For auld lang syne,*
> *We'll tak' a cup o' kindness yet*
>   *For auld lang syne.*

> *And surely ye'll be your pint stowp!**   *tankard
> *And surely I'll be mine!*
> *And we'll tak a cup o' kindness yet,*
>   *For auld lang syne.*

Chorus

> *We twa hae run about the braes,*
>   *And pou'd the gowans* fine;*   *large daisies
> *But we've wondered mony a weary fitt,*
>   *Sin' auld lang syne.*

Chorus

We twa hae paidl'd in the burn,
  Frae morning sun till dine;*   *dinner time
But seas between us braid* hae roar'd   *broad
  Sin' auld lang syne.

Chorus

And there's a hand, my trusty fiere!
  And gie's a hand o' thine!
And we'll tak a right gude willie-waught,
  For auld lang syne.

For auld lang syne, my jo,
  For auld lang syne,
We'll tak' a cup o' kindness yet
  For auld lang syne.

THE MORN'S MORNING

The party's over - the last guest has left and the chairman and organiser are left alone with their thoughts Throughout the evening both have been watching every detail of the proceedings (not necessarily worrying about things, but taking in every detail). Within themselves they will know whether the dinner has been a success or if certain aspects could be improved next year.

Naturally, they will discuss it with other people to find out their comments, but one thing they will never know — There is no way of finding out how many people went home inspired to open a copy of Burns and read it.

There is still work to be done though: speakers and entertainers no doubt were thanked verbally and publicly at the end of the evening, but each should be sent a brief letter of thanks. No doubt they had a good dinner and enjoyed themselves, but they did give up their time to attend *your* Burns Supper, and the club is in their debt at least to the extent of a letter of thanks. It costs a speaker time and trouble to attend a dinner, so never take his contribution for granted.

If the local newspapers have been unable to attend, send a brief report to them quickly, and of course, if the club is in membership of the Robert Burns World Federation (the Burns Federation) a report should be forwarded to the Editor of the *Burns Chronicle*.

Give some thought to how this should be worded. "Mr . . . proposed an eloquent Immortal Memory" may be true, but it tells those who were not present absolutely nothing about the event. Some organisers spread themselves and still say nothing. So give details of the speaker clearly and concisely, add a paragraph about the content of his speech, perhaps even a short quotation.

Before you send it off, read it, for goodness sake. After speaking at a Dinner once I was amused to read in the *Burns Chronicle*: "The Immortal Memory was proposed by Mr. Hugh Douglas, followed by some excellent speeches and entertainers." I am still trying to figure out whether the secretary meant what he wrote.

A committee meeting should be held soon after the Anniversary Dinner, not so much as an inquest as to capitalise on the enthusiasm generated by the Dinner to start work on the next one. This is the time to make reservations, find speakers and to engage singers for next year. It is also the time to plan the programme for the twelve months ahead.

The Burns Supper is only a small part of the year's activities for many clubs, the focal point of a programme which keeps Burns's work fresh in the minds of members.

Burns was a convivial man who would relish regular friendly meetings with plenty of companionship and laughter. This, much more than the formal dinner would please him, so regular meetings with talks, readings and discussions are a good basis for the Burns year. Visiting speakers from other clubs bring a fresh outlook on Burns and his works, and, or course, outings can be made to kindred clubs.

St. Andrews Night ought to be the other highlight of the year, and here Burns can be placed happily into the context of Scottish literary achievement. By showing the works of others - the balladmakers, Boswells and others of the 18th century, Scott, Stevenson, Buchan and the many fine modern poets of Scotland - Burns will be shown to have had unique talents which set him apart from all the others. It will also shine clearly through that, contrary to what many south of the Border think, Scotland is not a one-author country - her heritage is rich and deserves to be better appreciated. Burns ought to be used to display this and not merely to repeat his own talents again and again without relating them to anything or anyone else.

Burns must also be the basis for looking to the future. The Bard himself was a farsighted man, and this is why the Federation encourages work among young people through talks to schools and projects and competitions in schools with appropriate prizes of Burns's works Where there is an interested or a co-operative headmaster this work is achieving much to promote knowledge and interest. If there is no glowing spark in a school already, then it is up to the club to ignite one. Talk to teachers, offer to come and speak about Burns to the pupils, invite the headmaster to be a guest to your Dinner, and keep in touch with him about your club activities.

Perhaps one way of arousing interest in teachers is to show that Burns can help to create a wider interest in Scottish literature generally. Instead of a Burns competition run a general Scottish literature one, or one for writing in Scottish dialect. Always think broadly when promoting Burns, and you will come close to the Poet's own objectives.

Because the focus of the Burns cult is the Poet's birthday, Burns tends to be thought of as a man of winter. Nothing could be further from the truth: Burns's health deteriorated as winter fastened her grip on the Scottish landscape and his spirits ebbed until he was a mere shadow of his real self. Spring returned and the warming sun slowly restored his health and his spirits. In the bleak Scottish climate the process was a slow one, and he himself admitted that August had come before he was in song again. In 1796 the returning sun was too slow and Burns never recovered, He died in July that year.

At many places a ceremony is held to mark the poet's death, usually with a wreath-laying, but at Ayr a service is held at Leglen Wood and a new dimension has been brought to the movement by an annual Burns Festival, held throughout the Burns Country, consisting of talks, concerts and other activities. It is right that a summer festival should be associated with the Poet who was so much a man of that season.

This broadening of the Burns cult can never overshadow the 25th of January: Burns Night will always have a special meaning for Scots whether at home or in exile. To non-Scots the Burns Supper may appear at best something faintly comic and at worst a hard-drinking, haggis-eating night which turns the Dr Jekyll in the Scot into a Mr Hyde. A few Burns Suppers may deserve that description, but by and large the celebration is a serious one, to be taken earnestly even by those organisations which have no direct connection with Burns.

The Burns Supper means more to the Scot than any stranger can understand. A well-travelled Scot once summed it all up to me in a letter:

"It is when you are very far from home that a Burns Supper takes on a completely new form. One night in Melbourne many years ago, my father, a keen member of Melbourne Burns Club, brought home a starving man who had been working in the Outback for many months. We found out he was a Scot, called Tom Wilson, a weaver from Hawick, and having been fed and clothed Tom marched round the garden playing Common Riding songs on his bugle. Then out of his knapsack he took three books - a Bible, Lockhart's Life of Scott and Burns's Poems. With tears running down his cheeks he read his favourite, *The Cotter's Saturday Night*. My father's reward was to take Tom to the next Burns Supper where Tom was the star of the evening, next to Burns himself."

The twenty-fifth of January is one day of the year when the Scot returns to his roots; when he takes stock of himself. It is only right that the focus of this re-dedication should be the man who, more than any other, helped Scotland to retain her nationhood, her heritage and her native tongue. But Robert Burns no longer belongs to Scotland alone. He is a citizen of the whole world, a man who can express the feelings of all men and remind them of their finest qualities. He is the Poet who never lost sight of the brotherhood of man and he won't let us lose sight of it either.

Thus the Burns Supper has become more than a convivial gathering - convivial though it may be - It is a celebration with power to do immense good. Burns does not need the celebrations each 25 January to keep him alive: what he had to say and the way in which he expressed it is important enough to guarantee him immortality.

It is *we* who need Burns and the Burns Night celebration to remind us of all the good that is encapsulated in the Poet's works, and to live by the principles which he laid down.

THE ROBERT BURNS WORLD FEDERATION

(formerly The Burns Federation)
Headquarters: Dick Institute, Kilmarnock, KA1 3BU, 01563 572469.
Contact: Shirley Bell, Chief Administrator, or John Inglis.

To help you achieve all that has been suggested in the foregoing pages, the Robert Burns World Federation is there to lend a hand. Call on them if you need guidance, for there is one thing you can always be sure of - the Burnsian circle all round the globe is a friendly one, eager to share its knowledge and enthusiasm with anybody who is interested in the Bard.

When two Burns enthusiasts, walking along the Embankment in London following the unveiling of the statue of the Poet there in 1884, chatted casually about the idea of a bringing together all those who were interested in Robert Burns, they did not know what they were starting. Formed in Kilmarnock the following year, 1885, the organisation was named the Burns Federation, and it quickly took root. Its present title, the Robert Burns World Federation, reflects its global expansion over the years.

The Federation is dedicated to the memory of the Bard, and achieves this by encouraging both Burns Clubs and individuals to honour the poet's memory, and to strengthen the bond of fellowship between Burnsians everywhere. It also works to conserve places associated with Burns, and to promote Scotland and the Scots' literary heritage.

The Federation now has some 370 clubs in membership as well as over 400 individual members, and its work extends beyond the Bard to encourage the development of Scottish literature, art and music generally. Keeping the old Scottish tongue alive is another of its goals, and it assists young people to grow up to love their national heritage through competitions in schools. In short the Federation links past with present and preserves Scotland's heritage among men and women of Scottish descent all over the world.

The Federation, has produced the *Burns Chronicle* annually since 1892, a publication packed with Burns scholarship, comment on the Poet and his works, and information about the Burns movement worldwide.

THE BURNS SUPPER COMPANION
THE APT QUOTATION

Finding a quotation to illustrate an aspect of Burns can be daunting for the beginner. It is impossible to plough through hundreds of poems in the faint hope of discovering a suitable one so here is a list, by no means a complete one, of poems on a variety of subjects likely to be of help to speakers at Burns Suppers.

About his own life
There was a Lad
The Cotter's Saturday Night
To Willie Simpson
Epistles to Davie

Satire on religion and the Church
The Holy Tulzie
Holy Willie's Prayer
The Holy Fair
The Ordination
The Kirk's Alarm
The Twa Herds

Other Satires
Death and Doctor Hornbrook
The Twa Dugs
Address to the Deil

The Dignity and suffering of Man
Man was made to Mourn
On seeing a Wounded Hare
A Man's a Man for A' That

To a Mouse
The Twa Dogs

Patriotism
Scots Wha Hae
Does Haughty Gaul Invasion Threat

Jacobitism
A Highland Lad my love was born
Lines written at Stirling
   (Here Stewarts once in triumph reign'd)
The Bonnie Lass of Albanie
Up and Warn a' Willie
Hey Johnnie Cope
The White Cockade
   (My love was born in Aberdeen)
The Luvely Lass o' Inverness
Charlie he's my Darling

Love
I'm o'er young to marry yet
A Rosebud by my early walk
Of a' the airts
O were I on Parnassus Hill
Afton Water
The Lea Rig
O Whistle and I'll come to ye, my lad
My love she's but a Lassie yet
John Anderson, my Jo
Ye Banks and Braes o' Bonnie Doon
Ae Fond Kiss
Bonnie Wee thing
Willie Wastle

Drinking
Willie Brew'd a Peck o' Maut
The De'il's awa' wi' the Exciseman
John Barleycorn
Scotch Drink

Remembrance and Parting
Auld Lang Syne
Ae Fond Kiss

Some Useful Quotations which might be hard to find unless you know your way around Burns's poetry and song. The C.W. page reference refers to the page number on all of the editions of "The Complete Works of Robert Burns."

Then gently scan your brother man,
Still gentler sister woman;
Tho they may gang a kennin* wrang,   *little
To step aside is human:
Address to the Unco Guid ~ C.W. page 74

Auld Coila, now may fidge fu fain,*   *get excited
She's gotten bardies o' her ain;
Chiels wha their chanters winna hain,*   * spare
But tune their lays,
Till echoes a' resound again
Her weel-sung praise.
To William Simpson ~ C.W. page 107

'O Death! the poor man's dearest friend,
The kindest and the best!
Welcome the hour my aged limbs
Are laid with thee at rest!
Man was made to Mourn ~ C.W. page 123

The best-laid schemes o mice and men
Gang aft agley,*   *wrong
An lea'e us nought but grief an pain
For promis'd joy!
To a Mouse ~ C.W. page 131

Fortune! if thou'll but gie me still
Hale breeks,* a scone, an whisky gill,   *trousers
An rowth o rhyme to rave at will,
Tak a' the rest.
Scotch Drink ~ C.W. page 165

O wad some Power the giftie gie us
To see oursels as ithers see us!
It wad frae monie a blunder free us
An foolish notion.
To a Louse ~ C.W. page 181

But pleasures are like poppies spread,
You seize the flow'r, its bloom is shed;
Or like the snow falls in the river,
A moment white - then melts for ever;
Or like the borealis race,
That flit ere you can point their place;
Or like the rainbow's lovely form
Evanishing amid the storm.
Tam O Shanter ~ C.W. page 410

Nae man can tether time or tide.
Tam O Shanter ~ C.W. page 410

Had we never lov'd sae kindly,
Had we never lov'd sae blindly,
Never met - or never parted -
We had ne'er been broken-hearted.
Ae Fond Kiss ~ C.W. page 434

Then let us pray that come it may,
(As come it will for a' that),
That Sense and Worth, o'er a' the earth,
Shall bear the gree* an a' that.   *win first prize
A Man's a Man for a' That ~ C.W. page 535

The heart ay's the part ay,
That makes us right or wrang.
Epistle to Davie ~ C.W. page 86

I'm truly sorry man's dominion
Has broken Nature's social union.
To a Mouse ~ C.W. page 131

Man's inhumanity to man,
Makes countless thousands mourn!
Man was Made to Mourn ~ C.W. page 123

From scenes like these, old Scotia's grandeur springs,
That makes her lov'd at home, rever'd abroad:
Princes and lords are but the breath of kings,
"An honest man's the noblest work of god";
The Cotter's Saturday Night ~ C.W. page 147

Gie me ae spark o' Nature's fire,
That's a' the learning I desire;
First Epistle to John Lapraik ~ C.W. page 101

"The social, friendly, honest man,
Whate'er he be,
'Tis he fulfils great Nature's plan,
And none but he."
Second Epistle to John Lapraik ~ C.W. page 104

There's nought but care on ev'ry han',
In every hour that passes, O:
What signifies the life o' man,
An 'twere na for the lasses, O.
Green Grow the Rashes, O ~ C.W. page 81

Auld Nature swears, the lovely dears
Her noblest work she classes, O;
Her prentice han' she try'd on man,
An then she made the lasses, O.
Green Grow the Rashes, O ~ C.W. page 81

I was na fou,* but just had plenty.   *drunk
Death and Dr. Hornbrook ~ C.W. page 96

Farewell to the Highlands, farewell to the North,
The birthplace of valour, the country of worth!
Wherever I wander, wherever I rove,
The hills of the Highlands for ever I love.
My Heart's in the Highlands ~ C.W. page 390

If there's a hole in a' your coats,
I rede you tent* it;   *attend to
A chield's amang you, takin notes
And, faith, he'll prent it.
On the late Captain Grose's Peregrination
thro' Scotland ~ C.W. page 373

If there's another world, he lives in bliss;
If there is none, he made the best of this.
Epitaph on William Muir ~ C.W. page 70

Then at the balance let's be mute,
We never can adjust it.
What's done we partly may compute,
But know not what's resisted.
Address to the Unco Guid ~ C.W. page 74

But facts are chiels that winna ding,*   *won't be changed
And downa* be disputed   *cannot
A Dream ~ C.W. page 233

Some rhyme a neebor's name to lash;
Some rhyme (vain thought!) for needfu' cash;
Some rhyme to court the countra clash,*   *gossip
An raise a din:
For me, an aim I never fash;
I rhyme for fun.
Epistle to James Smith ~ C.W. page 169

BOOKS TO HELP YOU

BURNS'S WORKS

Burns' Poems and Songs. Edited by James Kinsley - Oxford University Press
Robert Burns. Penguin Poets - Penguin
The Complete Letters of Robert Burns. Edited by James A. Mackay - Alloway Publishing
The Complete Poetical Works of Robert Burns. Edited by James A. Mackay - Alloway Publishing

ABOUT ROBERT BURNS

Life of Robert Burns by Catherine Carswell - Chatto & Windus
Robert Burns: The Tinder Heart by Hugh Douglas - Sutton Publishing
Robert Burns, the Man and His Work by Hans Hecht - Alloway Publishing
The Burns Encyclopedia by Maurice Lindsay - Robert Hale
Life of Burns by J.G.Lockhart - J.M.Dent
Dirt & Deity: A Life of Robert Burns by Ian McIntyre - Harper/Collins
A Biography of Robert Burns by James Mackay - Mainstream Publishing
Robert Burns - Farmer by Gavin Sprott - National Museums of Scotland
Love & Liberty: Robert Burns a Bicentenary Celebration. Edited by Kenneth Simpson - Tuckwell Press
The Burns Chronicle. Published by the Robert Burns World Federation annually

ON JEAN ARMOUR AND OTHER WOMEN IN HIS LIFE

Jean Armour: Mrs Robert Burns (includes Sketches on Lives of Sarah Burns and Jessy Lewars) by Peter J. Westwood - Creedon Publications
Burns' Mrs Riddell by Angus Macnaghten - Volturna Press
Burns and Highland Mary by Yvonne Helen Stevenson - T. M. Gemmell

ABOUT SCOTLAND, ITS HISTORY AND CULTURE

A Short History of Scotland by R.L. Mackie - Penguin
The Lion in the North by John Prebble - Penguin
Scotland's Story by Tom Steel - Collins
The Haggis: A Little History by Clarissa Dickson Wright - Appletree Press
The Scots Kitchen by F. Marian McNeill - Mercat Press
Ena Baxter's Scots Cook Book by Ena Baxter - Johnstone & Bacon

ABOUT THE BURNS COUNTRY

The Ayrshire Book of Burns Lore by A.M. Boyle - Alloway Publishing
Discovering Ayrshire by John Strawhorn & Ken Andrew - John Donald
The Dumfriesshire Book of Burns Lore by James A. Mackay - Alloway Publishing

ABOUT SPEECH-MAKING IN GENERAL

Speaking in Public by Louise Bostock - Collins Pocket Reference series
Perfect Public Speaking by Paul McGee - Arrow Books
Debrett's Guide to Speaking in Public by Carole McKenzie - Headline Books
Bluff Your Way in Public Speaking by Chris Steward & Mike Wilkinson - Bluffer's Guide Series
Straightforward Guide to Public Speaking by Rosemary Riley - Straightforward Guides Series

DRINKS TO ACCOMPANY THE HAGGIS

We are na fou, we're nae that fou,
But just a drappie in our e'e!
The cock may craw, the day may daw,
And ay we'll taste the barley bree!

Willie brewed a peck o' maut, and Robert Burns and his friends spent a merry night enjoying it - they might well have washed down their haggis with it too, but I'm certain they didn't pour it into the haggis! Have you seen this custom at Burns Suppers of folk pouring whisky on to their haggis as if it were an essential, or even a traditional garnish for the dish? Well, take my word for it, it's neither, and it's a heathen custom that is a waste of good whisky and the ruination of a lovely haggis. Besides, there are plenty of other drinks which complement haggis, but don't pour any of them over it - just drink them as a ceremonial toast and then enjoy them as an accompaniment to the dish.

The haggis-makers, Macsween of Edinburgh, suggest you go down another alcoholic route for the haggis - drink whisky for the ceremonial toast, then a good red wine, ale, or even a Scottish fruit wine with it. Here are a few of their suggestions:

RED WINES Lighter Loire wines such as Saumur, Chinon, or Menetou Salon are good French reds which complement haggis well. Or try a Côtes du Rhône or Languedoc-Roussillon. But there are also excellent reds from Spain, Italy, Australia and California.

A Spanish Temperanillo, or Fuente del Ritmo or Montepulciano from Italy are good European choices. From Australia comes a Shiraz/Cabernet grape blend called Killawarra Shiraz Cabernet Sauvignon, or from California Redwood Trail, a Pinot Noir.

DRINKS TO GO WITH HAGGIS

WHITE WINES If you are a white wine *afficionado*, don't despair. But choose something dry and full enough to stand up well alongside haggis's distinctive taste. The Gewurtztraminer and Pinot Gris blends of Alsace would fit the bill, or so too would a Semillon/Chardonnay blend - there are some good ones from Australia around.

ALES Choose one that is rich, dark and able to hold its own alongside the 'beastie'. After all, this is what the folk drank in Burns' own time. It was home-made too, so what about a real ale from one of the many small real ale brewers that are around?

SCOTTISH FRUIT WINES It stands to reason that wines produced from the fruits of the countryside should blend well with the taste of haggis, and they are certainly different. Cairn o' Mohr winery at Errol in Perthshire, produce a variety, including raspberry and elderberry - But be warned, they are not innocent non-alcoholics!

OTHER DRINKS For non-alcohol drinkers a good quality dry, sharp apple juice enhances the haggis flavour. Or what about a glass of good old Scottish mineral water - on the rocks for preference!

 . . . AND OF COURSE THERE'S "THE DRAM"

The Dram has always played an important role in celebrating Burns Night. Just as we look to Burns to illuminate our spirit and remind us of our national heritage, so we take a dram to focus our attention on the present, bring the past more vividly to life and add a rosy glow to the future.

The whisky we drink now is, however, very different from that enjoyed by Burns - some of which may even have originated in the illicit stills which were the bane of his life and that of his fellow Excisemen.

In those early days 'uisge beatha' (the water of life which we know today as whisky) was distilled in Scotland by the local people for their own consumption. It would have been rough in comparison with the blends we enjoy today, little time being allowed for ageing and scant consideration given to the fact that it was probably comparatively impure.

But it was a popular and heart-warming drink among sturdy farming folk who took a jug of their own brew with them when visiting friends: This would be added to a communal container to be mixed with the whisky brought by other guests.

Although originally a Highland drink, by the time of the first Burns suppers (in the early 1800s) the popularity of whisky had begun to spread south to be enjoyed by Scots throughout the land - indeed throughout the world. Today we are spoilt for choice, for there is a range of blended and malt whiskies to please every palate, and you can be sure of one thing - they all wash the haggis down well!

Robert Burns, Poet
died 1796